MG Y-TYPE

This book is dedicated
to my father
Joseph J. Lawson

MG Y-TYPE

Saloons and Tourers

JOHN LAWSON

MOTOR RACING PUBLICATIONS LIMITED

MOTOR RACING PUBLICATIONS LIMITED
Unit 6, The Pilton Estate, 46 Pitlake, Croydon CR0 3RY, England

This work is published with the assistance of the Michael Sedgwick
Memorial Trust. Founded in memory of the famous motoring
researcher and author Michael Sedgwick (1926-1983), the Trust is a
registered charity to encourage new research and recording of
motoring history. Suggestions for future projects, and donations,
should be sent to the Honorary Secretary of the Michael Sedgwick
Memorial Trust, c/o the John Montagu Building, Beaulieu,
Hampshire SO4 7ZN, England.

ISBN 0 947981 31 4
First Published 1988

Write for a free complete catalogue of MRP books to
Motor Racing Publications Ltd, Unit 6, The Pilton Estate, 46 Pitlake,
Croydon CR0 3RY

Photoset by Tek-Art Ltd, West Wickham, Kent

Printed in Great Britain by
The Amadeus Press Ltd
Huddersfield, West Yorkshire

CONTENTS

INTRODUCTION   6

ACKNOWLEDGEMENTS   7

CHAPTER 1   Origins of the MG Y-type   9

CHAPTER 2   The Y-type saloon   15

CHAPTER 3   The YT tourer   35

CHAPTER 4   The YB saloon   43

CHAPTER 5   The XPAG engine   51

CHAPTER 6   Y-types in competition   57

CHAPTER 7   Y-type special bodies   61

CHAPTER 8   Buyer's guide   64

CHAPTER 9   Clubs, specialists and books   71

CHAPTER 10   Specifications   76

APPENDIX 1   Existing cars – important statistics   80

APPENDIX 2   List of all existing cars   81

APPENDIX 3   Points of originality & production figures   86

APPENDIX 4   Alternative part numbers listings   91

LUBRICATION CHARTS   107

CONTEMPORARY MAGAZINE REPORTS   109

INTRODUCTION

At some point between 1968 and the mid-seventies all the official factory production records relating to the M.G. 1¼-litre Saloon and Tourer were mislaid or destroyed. It has taken 10 years to reconstruct what is contained in these pages. (Perhaps this may serve, among other things, as an object lesson in the importance of preserving documentation wherever feasible, however unimportant it may seem at the time, in order to record our heritage.) Unfortunately, I doubt very much whether it will ever be possible to supply original production data for every individual car which left the Abingdon factory. Nevertheless, what follows will, I trust, be of value and interest to all Y-type owners, would-be owners, and those who are simply anxious to know more about these models which have hitherto been among the most overlooked products of the celebrated M.G. company.

John G. Lawson

ACKNOWLEDGEMENTS

For valuable help and encouragement, thanks to D. Ransome, G. Mills, A. Taylor, H. Nyncke, B. Leurink, C. Dye, D. Mullen, J. DeBoer, D. Ardill, T.J. Austin, D.H. Miller, T. Boscarino, J.N. Hancock, R. Gay, R. Knudson, T. Bowman, A.D. Clausager, R. Wonnacott, G.G. Werbizky, A. Albert, M.K. Wood, R. Wilson, J.L. Shaw, J.S.R. Bridges, J. Dawes, H.W. Chapman, R. Lowry, E. Kengelbacher, F. Adam, R. Jesson, R. Stormes, R.J. Andrews, W. Stocker, B. Mellem, R. Monk, L.C. Morriss, N. Mort, D.R. Lawrence, E. Turner, R.J. Hamilton, K.J. Richardson, Mrs Charlotte Luer, M.W. Dodd, The M.G. Owners' Club, The Octagon Car Club, Castrol, British Motor Industry Heritage Trust, The M.G. Car Club, The New England M.G. T Register, The Australian T Series Association.

Journals consulted in the course of research include *Motoring, Automobile Engineer, Autocar, Motor, Motor Trader, Wheelspin, The Sacred Octagon, Restored Cars, Motor Industry, Motorsport, Safety Fast, The Sunday Times, M.G. Magazine, Enjoying M.G., Motoring & Leisure*.

Books which have shed light on various aspects of the Y-type story include:

The Morris Car 1913-1983 by Harry Edwards.

M.G. by McComb by Wilson McComb.

The T-Series M.G.s by Graham Robson.

The Immortal T Series by Chris Harvey.

An Illustrated History of Rallying by Graham Robson.

The Jaguar XJS by Rivers Fletcher.

Tuning & Maintenance of M.G. Cars by Philip H. Smith.

Jaguar – Britain's Fastest Export by Lord Montagu of Beaulieu.

An M.G. Experience by Dick Jacobs.

The Art of Abingdon by John Mclellan.

Morris 8 Series E & Morris 10 Series M Owners' Handbooks (Nuffield Press).

The Austin-Rover Group Archives.

Grateful thanks to all the members of The M.G. Y-type Register past and present.

Lastly, to anyone I have forgotten, I do apologise.

J.G.L.

Safety fast!

CHAPTER 1

Origins of the MG Y-type

The story of M.G. was for many years one of close association with Morris products. M.G. started life as the Morris Garages, a collection of showrooms, depots and workshops located in Oxford and owned by Sir William Richard Morris (later Lord Nuffield). The first M.G.s were modified Morris cars, but until 1935 the M.G. Car Company Ltd (as it had become by that time) and Morris Motors Ltd were separate companies, although both were owned by Sir William. In 1935, following a takeover, the M.G. Car Company Ltd was brought under the umbrella of the Nuffield Organisation (which also owned Wolseley) and from then on commonality with and derivation from Morris and Wolseley (and later BMC) products was to be a part of life at M.G.

By mid-1937 the much-rationalized M.G. range featured two saloons, the SA (with a 2,288cc or 2,322cc six-cylinder engine) and the four-cylinder VA, or 1½-Litre (at 1,548cc). These cars were very much Wolseley-derived. The larger 2,561cc WA was to follow late in 1938 and, together, the S, V and W-range cars were seen by M.G. as effective competition to the products then being offered by S.S. (later to become Jaguar) Cars Ltd. Meanwhile, Morris had introduced the 10 Series M saloon during 1938 and at the Earls Court Motor Show on October 13 that year the smaller 8 Series E was shown for the first time.

The next step was for the Nuffield Organisation to look for a smaller saloon which would be a natural extension of M.G.'s current S, V and W range but would compete with the products being offered at the time by Triumph, Singer and Riley and the Rootes Group's Sunbeam-Talbots. All prototypes emanating from the design offices of M.G.'s Abingdon-on-Thames factory were allocated numbers prefixed by the letters EX until the mid-fifties, and although the prototype of what was to become the 1¼-Litre M.G. saloon was designed at the Morris factory at Cowley (it was the first M.G. the design of which was not the work of the company's founder, Cecil Kimber) it was, nevertheless, allocated the designation EX.166.

The prototype Y-type M.G., or M.G. Ten as it was known initially, was constructed in 1939 for launch at the 1940 Earls Court Motor Show and was therefore to have been a 1941 model. Unfortunately, the war intervened and it was not until 1947 that Abingdon could begin production of a car which was very little altered from the 1939 mock-up. Some evidence has since come to light to suggest that there were actually two EX.166 prototypes and that one, at least, was fully drivable. Neither, however, appears to have survived for long after the war.

EX.166 featured an independent front suspension layout designed by Alec Issigonis (later of Morris Minor and Mini fame) and Jack Daniels (an ex-M.G. draughtsman) for fitment to the

Known as the 2-Litre, this 1936 SA four-door saloon was based extensively on Wolseley components and, in fact, had an engine capacity of more than 2.2 litres, later extended to over 2.3 litres.
Pic: J.G. Lawson

A development of the SA saloon, this is a 1938 2.6-Litre, designated the WA, which was also largely Wolseley-based. No further cars this large were destined to carry the M.G. badge.
Pic: J.G. Lawson

prewar Morris 10 Series M saloon. As the system did not in fact appear on the Morris on grounds of cost, the Y-type was to become one of the first British production cars to be fitted with independent front suspension. At Abingdon, Sydney Enever, who for some years previously had been involved with the development of independent suspension systems for M.G's racing cars, also worked with Issigonis on adapting the latter's system for use on the Y. At the time, this independent coil-and-wishbone front suspension system was very advanced and later it was to be fitted to a whole range of BMC cars, only being phased out with the demise of the MGB in 1980. The Y also employed rack-and-pinion steering, the first

Nuffield product to be so equipped.

A modified Morris 8 Series E bodyshell in pressed steel (designed by Gerald Palmer) was chosen for the new M.G. saloon, but with the addition of a swept tail and rear wings. Whereas the Morris 10 Series M had incorporated the latest unitary construction techniques, the 8 Series E had a separate chassis. Strangely, though, the Wolseley 10 also had a separate chassis and both these designs were overslung in Morris tradition (that is to say the chassis curved up and over the back axle). For the Y-type, a completely new underslung chassis was developed which, interestingly, was later to lead to an overslung development of the same

Something of a 'halfway house' between the six-cylinder SA and WA saloons and the postwar 1¼-Litre, the 1½-Litre VA, which was also produced in drophead coupe and open tourer forms, considerably strengthened M.G.'s position as a manufacturer of up-market four-seater cars.
Pics: Sandy Taylor & J.G. Lawson

The Morris 8 Series E four-door saloon, of which the car above is a 1948 model, provided the basic body-shell pressings for the M.G. Y-type, while the Morris 10 Series M, seen on the left with its prewar design of radiator grille, was the source of the four-cylinder engine which would power the Y-type as well as many of its other mechanical components.

Pics: M.W. Dodd & P. Weale

These photographs, taken in 1939, show the EX.166 prototype for the car which originally was expected to be called the M.G. Ten, but which eventually came to market after the Second World War as the 1¼-Litre.

Pics: The British Motor Industry Heritage Trust – Austin Rover Group

chassis for the TD sports car. The engine which would power the Y-type, or 1¼-Litre M.G. as it was more properly called, was the 1,250cc XPAG unit which, first fitted to the TB sports car in 1939, had been developed from the Morris 10 Series M 1,140cc XPJM power unit introduced in the autumn of 1938.

Contemporary photographs of EX.166 show that the instrumentation was very basic and was similar to existing layouts in Morris saloons of the time (circular instrument dials in an apparently metal dashboard). In production, the Y-type was to be much more up-market, having a walnut veneered dashboard and the traditional octagonally shaped instrument faces (the instruments themselves remained circular but were placed behind octagonally shaped cut-outs in the wooden instrument panel to achieve the desired effect). The substitution of the traditional M.G. bonnet and grille for those of one or other of the contemporary Morris saloons emphasized the identity of the product, and the only other major alteration from prototype stage to production car was that EX.166 had much larger, squared-off, boot and spare wheel compartment lids than those of the Y-types when they eventually appeared in production.

Production of the Y began early in 1947 with chassis number Y 0251 (251 being the factory telephone number). Officially, there never was a YA, although throughout the remainder of this book I have chosen, in the main, to refer to the initial production version of the Y-type as the YA because over the years this designation found favour amongst owners and enthusiasts and its use will therefore avoid possible confusion.

CHAPTER 2

The Y-type saloon

The 1¼-Litre M.G. (Series Y) cars which began to emerge from the Abingdon-on-Thames factory in the spring of 1947 were an amalgam of traditional British craftsmanship and vehicle building practice and innovation in both bodywork construction and mechanical specification. The separate chassis and body, the interior of the latter employing an abundance of leather and wood, were a reminder of the best coachbuilding traditions, whereas the pressed-steel body construction, rather than the earlier technique of applying steel or aluminium panels to a wooden frame, and the use of independent front suspension and rack-and-pinion steering were moves towards the more modern approach to passenger car design.

The Y-type's newly designed chassis incorporated longitudinal 4¼in x 2⅝in spot-welded box-sections between the axles, joined by four crossmembers, and was made from 14G steel. This was a far cry from the chassis of the early T Series (TA, TB and TC) sports cars which had gone before, and provided a significant improvement in terms of rigidity and handling. The engine and gearbox were mounted fairly well forward in this chassis to give good weight distribution and at the same time bring the rear seating within the wheelbase.

Allied to the rigid chassis was the Issigonis-inspired independent front suspension which incorporated lateral wishbones and coil springs. The lower wishbone axes were parallel and there was no camber at normal load. This configuration would help enormously when checks had to be made to the chassis and allied components for accident damage. The upper links of the suspension were each formed by the double arms of a new and improved design of Luvax Girling piston-type damper. Similar shock absorbers, in this case fitted with single lever arms, were employed at the rear of the car.

The helical direct-acting rack-and-pinion steering was contained in a housing attached at two points to the front crossmember. The outer ball joints were attached to steering levers which linked the steering to the front suspension whilst the inner ball joints were contained within rubber end gaiters which restrained the lubricating oil which serviced the rack and inner ball joints.

At the rear of the car, a spiral-bevel banjo-type axle, almost identical to that fitted to the Morris 10 Series M, was supported by semi-elliptic leaf springs and located by a transverse radius or Panhard rod which was deemed essential for good handling. Transmission to the back axle was by means of a Hardy Spicer tubular propshaft with needle-roller universal joints, which took the drive from a four-speed gearbox with synchromesh on second, third and top. The 7¼in diameter Borg & Beck clutch was connected to the pedal mechanism by Bowden cable.

The Lockheed hydraulic braking system employed 9in drums front and rear, the shoes being adjusted by snail cam adjusters actuated by the application of a screwdriver through holes in the drum without removal of the road wheel being necessary. The cable-operated handbrake acted on the two rear wheels from a lever mounted on the propshaft tunnel between the front seats. The 3.00in x 16in wheels, which were fixed by five studs, carried 5.00/5.25 x 16in tyres. The car was supplied with an 8-gallon fuel tank, which was fed from a filler in the nearside rear wing.

A most useful feature of the chassis design was the self-contained Jackall hydraulic jacking system. This had been fitted to a number of cars before the war (including the S, V and W M.G.s) as original equipment and was to continue to be fitted to several of the more up-market offerings and some commercial vehicles into the early fifties. The system was an optional extra on the Morris 10 Series M but was standard on the Y-type M.G. and Wolseley 10. Four hydraulically-actuated rams, the rear two being attached one either side of the car to the rear axle, enabled the driver to raise either the front, the rear, or the whole of the car high enough

One of the first XPAG/SC engines being lowered into position on a YA chassis at Abingdon early in 1947.
Pic: The British Motor Industry Heritage Trust – Austin Rover Group

16

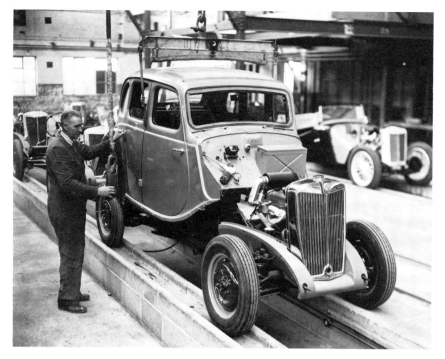

off the ground to facilitate a wheel change simply by applying lever action to a junction box on the nearside of the car under the bonnet. On the prewar M.G. saloons and the Wolseley 10 the junction box had been mounted beneath the floorboards with access from within the car.

The six-light four-door saloon body of the Y-type M.G. was very much that of the Morris 8 Series E with minor modifications. The Wolseley Eight, of which approximately 4,000 were made, also utilized a slightly modified version of this bodyshell. The body was attached by three bolts each side to the chassis brackets, by a further two bolts each side at the extreme rear and by two additional bolts each side to the scuttle stay brackets. One setscrew on each side in the rear corners of the bonnet valance completed the fixings.

The body contained provision for an exterior-opening luggage compartment and a separate compartment located under the boot floor to house the spare wheel and tools. It should be remembered that before the war the fashion in general and particularly in respect of Nuffield saloons was to have no external opening to the boot, all luggage being loaded from inside the car and stowed behind the seats. For the carriage of bulky loads, facilities existed for owners to fit two leather or webbing straps which would hang down from inside the boot compartment; these could be unrolled and fitted over luggage carried on the open bottom-hinged bootlid.

Both front and rear seats were leather-covered (Connolly hide) on wearing surfaces with Rexine (leathercloth) backs and side pieces. The rear seat employed a fold-down centre armrest and, to aid the rear passengers' exit from the armchair-like rear seats, loop-type grab straps were fitted just above and to the front of the two fixed rear side windows. The door trim panels were in leathercloth, with real leather sewn-on map pockets. Black carpet covered the wooden floorboards. The dashboard, facia and instrument panel were of wood with walnut veneered exterior surfaces and incorporated two basic instruments, five switches and a glove compartment, whilst the headlining in all cars was beige-coloured Union Melton cloth.

The position of each front seat was adjustable, as was the length of the steering column, and a toggle above the driver's door (next to the interior light switch) operated the rear window blind by means of a long cord. It may be said that, given the fact that standard equipment

One of the oldest Y-types still in existence today is this car with the chassis no. Y 0296. It is based in Virginia, USA, where it is known by the nickname Penelope.

Pic: W.L. Genther

A typical example of a two-tone YA saloon. In this instance the bulk of the body is finished in a light metallic Almond Green with wings and wheels sprayed in the darker Shires Green.

Pic: Sandy Taylor

included only one very small interior rear-view mirror and no wing mirrors, the raising of the rear window blind would effectively reduce rearward visibility to nil! The key for the spare wheel compartment lid was tucked through a loop of leathercloth down by the front passenger's left knee (perhaps suggesting that he or she should get out and help the driver change a wheel should the need arise!).

A sliding sunroof and opening windscreen added quite superbly to the variety of ventilation which could be enjoyed whilst, in more inclement weather, the electrically powered windscreen wipers could be operated independently, or even by hand, by means of control knobs located on the wooden facia above the dashboard. A knurled ring incorporating a self-cancelling time-switch fitted to the centre of the steering wheel controlled the semaphore arms which were positioned between front and rear doors. The front and rear doors shared common centrally located hinges.

Externally, the bonnet opened longitudinally via a centre hinge, giving excellent access to all the major engine ancilliaries, while 8in chrome headlamps and a traditional vertical all-chrome M.G. radiator grille served to emphasize that this was indeed a very different car from the Morris 8 Series E from which the body was derived. Front and rear wings and running boards all bolted on to the basic pressed-steel bodyshell.

The first Y-types off the line in 1947 cost £671, a considerable proportion of which was Purchase Tax. When the owner took delivery of his new car he would find in it a red-covered

Nearside and offside views of a YA equipped with the central battery box. Everything is original in this engine bay with the exception of the addition of an accessory appropriate to the period – a Lucas windscreen washer complete with glass water reservoir.
Pics: J.G. Lawson

A superb restoration of a
1951 YA, which was carried
out by Chris Cridland,
of Leicestershire. Mounted
on the bulkhead is the
valve box for the period
radio fitted to this car.
Pic: J.G. Lawson

A modern restoration pro-
ject, but this is what the
B281 pressed-steel body
must have looked like
before it left Nuffield Metal
Products in Birmingham
en route to Abingdon.
Pic: D.C. Beidler

This bare YA chassis is not completely to original specification because its owner has fitted a YB front anti-roll bar to improve handling.

Pic: D.C. Beidler

Owners' Handbook and a similarly bound 18-page booklet entitled *The First 500 Miles on your new M.G. 1¼-Litre*. This latter publication gave advice on running-in and lubrication, etc and, when the first 500 miles had been completed, the owner was supposed to return the booklet to the factory, whence he would receive an official *Workshop Manual*. This explains why nowadays these booklets are very rare indeed. Additionally, a comprehensive toolkit was supplied as standard with each car.

Initially, cars were produced in black, grey or a two-tone grey-and-black scheme, but a little later they also appeared in overall green, a two-tone green and maroon. Sales brochures of the time were not always as accurate as those of today and a good deal of artistic licence was

The original interior of this car is slightly worn with age, but it has not been seriously damaged. Many Y-types are still to be found in this serviceable condition.

Pic: Mike Lewis

allowed. For example, brochures often offered Y-types in colours or colour combinations which never saw the light of day on actual vehicles. Throughout the production run of the Y, or YA as it later came to be known, official colour schemes which actually appeared were:

Exterior	Upholstery
Shires Green (a dark green)	Dark Green with beige piping. Beige with brown piping.
Shires Green/Elizabeth Grey (two-tone)	Beige with brown piping. Dark Green with beige piping.
Shires Green/Almond Green (two-tone)	Dark Green with beige piping. Beige with brown piping.
Almond Green (a medium green metallic)	Beige with brown piping. Dark Green with beige piping.
Autumn Red (a maroon)	Dark Red with beige piping. Beige with brown piping.
Black	Dark Red with beige piping. Beige with brown piping.
Elizabeth Grey (a light grey)	Dark Green with beige piping. Beige with brown piping. Dark Red with beige piping.
Elizabeth Grey/Black (two-tone)	Beige with brown piping.
Cream	Dark Red with beige piping. Dark Green with beige piping. Beige with brown piping.
Sun Bronze (a metallic)	Dark Red with beige piping. Beige with brown piping.

It was becoming accepted practice for names of certain colour shades to be changed for advertising purposes over a period of time, even though the shades themselves did not change. For instance, Autumn Red became Regency Red, Ivory became Sequoia Cream, etc.

A few words here about the various two-tone schemes may be opportune. The black/grey version featured wings and running boards finished in black with the remainder of the body in Elizabeth Grey. Likewise, the two-tone green scheme consisted of wings and running boards in the darker Shires Green whilst the body was in the lighter Almond Green. It might at first seem to the reader that it would have been more aesthetically pleasing to divide the two contrasting colours along the natural coachline of the body. The reason why the men at Abingdon did not adopt this approach was simple. While producing Shires Green cars and Almond Green cars and black ones and grey ones it was the easiest thing in the world (and a lot less expensive) to just bolt on a set of black wings and running boards to a grey car, for example. This practice had started at Abingdon in the mid-thirties with the P-series cars and had its origins, no doubt, in the Morris practice of always fitting black wings and running boards no matter what the colour of the car body was to be. The tradition continued on a much smaller scale after the war. It must also not be forgotten that M.G. were very sensitive to the wishes of their customers and 'special orders' were relatively common even after the war in the atmosphere of production-line conformity.

One such anomaly which has come to light concerns Y 0672. This car, which still exists

The instrument panel and dashboard of a YA saloon. The instruments themselves are circular, though recessed behind octagonal cut-outs in M.G. tradition. Spring-spoke steering wheels were considered an up-market feature at the time.

Pic: J.G. Lawson

The instrument panel of one of the very rare left-hand drive YA saloons. Note that the speedometer has been calibrated in kilometres per hour.

Pic: R. Schweiger

23

today, has a body finished in Elizabeth Grey and wings and running boards in British Racing Green (a shade significantly darker than M.G.'s own Shires Green). It also has chromium-plated twin wind-tone horns either side of the radiator grille. These features are known by the current owner to have been fitted at the factory as the car has been in his family all its life; his grandfather, who was the car's first owner, was the sales and service manager for Morris Motors at the time.

In the late forties/early fifties very little was offered by the motor manufacturers in the way of optional extras, but throughout the production life of the YA certain items were fitted to special order and often for export markets. The Sun Bronze metallic colour finish was in the main reserved for export cars, although quite a few cars were delivered in the UK in this scheme. Sun Bronze cars also tended to appear with optional extras such as a radio *or* a heater, an additional spotlamp and, in very few cases, over-riders fitted to the bumper blades. Cars finished in cream seem to have been made exclusively for export.

This YA, chassis no. Y 0672, was supplied new in the non-standard colour scheme of Elizabeth Grey with British Racing Green wings. Also to special order were the twin chromed WT614 horns mounted either side of the radiator grille.

Pic: F.J. Blick

It should also be borne in mind that shades of, for instance, Shires Green will have varied somewhat from year to year throughout the production run as new bulk quantities of the paint were made up and used. There was not at that time the strict control of paint specifications which exists in the motor industry today.

Type B281 bodies (those for the saloons) were assembled at the Nuffield Metal Products plant in Birmingham. They were, after all, basically Morris 8 Series E bodyshells and vast numbers of these were built both before and after the Second World War. Saloon upholstery in all probability originated at Cowley and it is thought that the sunroof panels were already trimmed when they arrived at Abingdon.

When private car production resumed after the Second World War the emphasis was very

One of the very best original Y-types still in the UK is this 1950 example owned by Trevor Austin, from Purley, Surrey. The 'UMG' registration number is evidence that the car was supplied by University Motors.

Pic: T.J. Austin

much on exporting so as to earn foreign currency and help the country recover from the war effort. Steel was strictly rationed and Sir Stafford Cripps, the President of the Board of Trade, had indicated firmly that supplies would be directed to those companies with the better export prospects. Between the end of 1945, when production of the TC sports car had started at Abingdon, and the spring of 1947, when the Y-type was introduced, it had become clear that the sports car was becoming an enormous export success. Although it was unlikely that the saloon would sell as well in export markets as the TC, at the time Great Britain had virtually a captive market in its ex-Empire countries whereas continental Europe had been more severely devastated by the war and was not yet in a position to recommence manufacture of private motor vehicles.

Australia was by far the largest export market for the Y-type saloon and today many still exist in the benign climate around Melbourne. A perusal of Abingdon's export statistics reveals that approximately 51% of all YAs produced were exported and it is a little-known fact that between 1948 and 1951 a handful of left-hand-drive YAs were produced. Six are known to exist today; three in the USA and three in the Netherlands.

An open tourer version of the Y-type M.G. was produced in 1948 and full details of this appear in the next chapter. However, it was because of the introduction of the tourer and the

Several owners have finished their cars in the M.G. 'house colours' of brown and cream, even though this was not an original colour finish for Y-types. This is Colin Lloyd's car, Y 6381, undergoing restoration in Geelong, Australia.

Pic: C.S. Lloyd

This is another example of a 'Cream Cracker' finish of brown and cream, in this instance a UK-based car.

Pic: N.W. Went

Two examples of Y-types with their Jackall System hydraulic jacking equipment in use. Please refer to the text for precautions which should be taken when operating these built-in jacks.

Pics: Sandy Taylor & S.E. Mitchell

need to produce the car in both RHD and LHD forms that the position of the battery box in the engine compartment was moved from the nearside (left-hand side) of the scuttle to a central position. This, in turn, facilitated the production of those few LHD saloons. No doubt the change to a common type of bulkhead with a centrally-mounted battery box was additionally made easier by the withdrawal from production, in 1948, of both the Morris 8 Series E and the Wolseley Eight. The last YA produced with an off-set battery box was Y 4459 in early 1950 (by that time the supply of early-type scuttle panels had dried up). **Fig 1** gives more extensive details of the technical changes made to YA saloons between 1947 and 1951.

Early sales brochures (this is the front cover of the catalogue produced for the YA in 1947) were mostly printed using single-colour artwork and line drawings.

Pic: J.G. Lawson

It is seldom that one sees original-type over-riders on YAs, but this car had them already fitted when it was delivered from the factory.

Pic: J.G. Lawson

An immaculately presented 1948 YA, chassis no. Y 1805, owned by Charles 'Skip' Kelsey, of Pleasanton, California.

Pic: Charles F. Kelsey

A line-up of well-preserved Y-types in California. The car on the extreme left is the well-known supercharged 1947 model once owned by Al Moss, founder of the US spares specialists Moss Motors.

Pic: R. Schweiger

Although not original, this California-based YA, which is finished in a two-tone black and dark red colour scheme, is an attractive-looking Y-type.
Pic: Tory Skopecek

At home, long waiting lists for new cars were developing. It was becoming quite easy for the owner of a new car to offer his car for sale immediately after delivery and receive a significantly higher sum for it on the 'secondhand' market than that which he had just paid to the manufacturer. To attempt to curb this it became necessary for the new owner to sign a covenant between himself, the Motor Traders Association and the dealer in which he undertook not to re-sell the car within six months without the approval of the MTA. The period during which sale was restricted, as covered by this type of covenant, increased over the years and by 1952 had reached two years! However, it was phased out completely in late 1952.

An example of what painstaking work can accomplish on a car which was once in a very sad state indeed is this YA, now finished in Almond Green. In its original state the car carried the registration number OKX 355.
Pic: K. Smith

Certainly one of the best restored YAs in Britain, this is Chris Cridland's car and is seen here at Brighton at the end of the Regency Run in May 1985.

Pic: J.G. Lawson

It would be hard to better the condition of this beautiful two-tone green 1948 YA, another car which was originally supplied through University Motors.

Pic: Source unknown

This is Paul Acfield's black 1948 YA from Melbourne, Australia, which carries the chassis no. Y 1175. It was photographed at a concours in Melbourne in December 1981.

Pic: P. Acfield

This interesting YA, which is finished in two only slightly different shades of red, was seen at Brighton on the occasion of the 1985 Regency Run.

Pic: J.G. Lawson

The motoring press of the time (primarily *The Autocar, The Motor* and *Motor Sport*) were on the whole in agreement that the new 1¼-Litre saloon from M.G. was mechanically very innovative and was a delight to drive. The positive action of the gearbox was repeatedly singled out for praise. The interior, they said, retained all that was best of traditional British craftsmanship and was functional and comfortable (except, perhaps, for long-legged rear seat passengers). All-round visibility was good and it was possible to cruise all day at 55mph without any problem! On the whole, the road testers liked the car very much.

By late 1951, when production gave way to the updated YB model, 6,158 YA saloons had been produced and the cost, including Purchase Tax, of a new example had risen to £880. Inflation was beginning to take hold as never before!

Y-types have a habit of collecting nicknames. This one is called Prudence and it belongs to Mr & Mrs H.J. Luer, of Denville, New Jersey.
Pics: J.G. Lawson

Fig 1	SERIES Y – SPECIFICATION CHANGES
From chassis no.	Details of modification.
Y 0535	Engine block and bulkhead colour changed from a greyish green to a darker shade of grey-green.
Y 0584	Voltage control regulator changed from RF91 to RF95/2.
Y 1261	New type of steering column slip-ring fitted together with a channel for the trafficator cable on the steering column and associated parts.
Y 1352	Engine block colour changed to maroon.
Y 1378	Distance tube introduced for clip on nearside brake pipe to rear axle.
Y 1625	Bulkhead colour became that of the individual car body finish.
Y 3627	Steering gearbox ball housings (male and female); shims (.003in and .005in) for ball seat and rack housing adaptor.
Y 4460	New type of petrol tank to fuel pump feed pipe. New starter and choke control knobs and associated apparatus (previously push-button starter; replaced by pull-out type). Wiring loom change associated with above. Stiffener for Jackall distributor box introduced on change-over to centrally-placed battery box (Y 4459 was last car with off-set battery box). Dashboard sound-deadening liner; anti-drum felt for gearbox and ramp plate LH and RH.
Y 4760	7in replaced 8in diameter headlamps.
Y 5011	Different type of fog lamp introduced.
Y 5420	Hub caps with centre MG medallion introduced.
Y 6165	Grease nipple for rear axle.
Y 6611	Further change in headlamp specification (still 7in).

Another view of the car pictured on the previous page, this time in the company of a TD M.G. in a typical rural setting in New England during the fall.
Pic: J.G. Lawson

CHAPTER 3

The YT tourer

As we shall see in a later chapter, early in 1948 at least three Y-type chassis had been treated to very neat open tourer bodies by the Swiss coachbuilding firm of Reinbolt & Christé S.A. The appearance of these cars may have had some influence upon M.G. themselves for, at the Earls Court Motor Show of October 1948, they introduced their own factory-produced four-seat open tourer version of the Y-type.

The YT, as the tourer was to be known, cost £525 when it was announced and was powered by a version of the XPAG engine which used twin semi-downdraught S.U. carburettors and the camshaft fitted to the TC sports car, and consequently it developed 54.5bhp compared to the 46bhp of the saloon. The YT weighed approximately 365lb more than the similarly-powered TC and approximately 84lb less than the Y saloon. A top speed of 76mph was deemed attainable as against the figure of 70mph in respect of the saloon. The tourer was to be offered for export only and, as such, provision had to be made for easy adaptation to LHD controls on the production line. As well as the relocation of the battery box which, from the owner's point of view, made access to the battery more difficult, the oil pump was modified so that it did not foul the LHD steering column and a different type of oil bath air cleaner was fitted to provide more efficient air filtration in dust-laden atmospheres abroad.

The YT was not simply a 'saloon with the roof chopped off', it was of significantly different construction. The doors (only two of them) were coachbuilt (that is to say, steel panels were fastened on wooden frames) and were deeply cut-away. The dashboard and instrument panel were peculiar to the model and incorporated a 5in diameter rev-counter directly in front of the driver and a similar-size speedometer in front of the front seat passenger. This arrangement used to be traditional and was supposed to convey the meaning that any driver worth his salt would, and indeed should, drive by reference to the rev-counter alone, instinctively knowing his road speed at the indicated revs! Between the two large instruments were arranged three smaller dials (ammeter, oil pressure gauge and fuel gauge) and the ignition and lighting switch. Indeed, the arrangement was very similar to the TC set-up; the wiring consisted of virtually a TC loom for the instrument panel connected to an almost standard YA saloon loom for the rest of the car. There were no direction indicators save on the Y/T/EX(U) cars for certain states of the USA.

Type B282 bodies (those for YTs) were assembled at Abingdon. YT upholstery also originated at Abingdon and, as indicated in the table below, there were different shades and colour combinations from those applicable to the saloons. Tourers had narrower rear seat

This YT, pictured before restoration began, reveals the fundamentals of the basic B282-type body.
Pic: A.W. Nuttall

A rare bird. This is one of the small number of YTs to be found in the UK, and well worth the hard work which clearly is necessary to bring it back to pristine condition.
Pics: J.G. Lawson

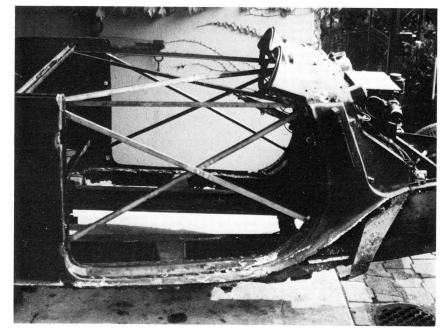

cushions to allow for the wide trim pads into which the hood and hood irons folded away. The rear cushions did not have the wing-like protruberences at the front end as on the saloons' rear seats. In addition, the front seats tilted forward to allow access to the rear seats. The rear window of the hood was removable and was secured by zip fasteners and, when folded and tucked away behind and at the sides of the rear seat, the hood and its associated equipment was zipped up neatly out of sight. The windscreen of the YT folded flat and the car had an unusually rigid body structure for an open tourer. It was reported that scuttle and door movement was nearly non-existent.

The YT was one of the last four-seat open tourers to be produced. This concept had been quite popular before the war, though, and there were high hopes for the car in that it provided open-top motoring for a family of four. The introductory report on the YT, published by *The Autocar* on October 8, 1948, stated that it had been designed primarily for the American

The instrument layout and dashboard of the YT echoes that of the TC sports car, with speedometer and rev-counter in front of the passenger and driver respectively. The right-hand drive car was pictured when undergoing restoration in Australia.

*Pics: D. Ardill &
G.G. Werbizky*

market. It went on to give the impression that all cars were to be produced in LHD layout and made much of the 'new-fangled' flashing direction indicator system introduced for the American market. If, however, one reads the report published by *The Motor* on October 13 it becomes clear that *The Autocar*'s article unfortunately contained sufficient inaccuracies to suggest that the writer had prepared his report, not from first-hand observation of an actual tourer, but possibly from M.G. press releases and conversations with uninformed parties

This beautiful YT belongs to Chris Green, of Thursford, Norfolk. It is one of the very few road-worthy YTs in the UK and is finished in an immaculate bright red.
Pic: C.B. Green

This picture of a two-tone Michigan-based YT illustrates the arrangement of the hood irons. The owner has fitted Morris Minor over-riders to the rear bumper, these being somewhat similar to the now very difficult to obtain original items.
Pic: B. Havel

(although the prototype YT *is* thought to have been LHD). Whilst it was true that a system of flashing indicators was introduced on cars destined for *certain* states of the USA, it must also be the case that the Nuffield Organisation knew that Australia rather than the USA would provide most of the demand for the YT. Indeed, the biggest proportion of YTs produced were RHD versions, including many of those that went to the USA, and comparatively few were produced with the flashing direction indicator system installed.

The hood cover sits neatly around the rear seat backrest of this YT, and the front passenger seat hinges forward in one piece to provide easy access to the rear compartment through the wide door opening.

Pics: G.G. Werbizky

This YT, which resides in Florida, USA, has at some time acquired chrome strips along the bonnet sides and curving down on to the doors. The car also has non-original TD-type over-riders on the front bumpers.

Pic: G.T. Banister

To reflect the more sporty outlook, tourers were finished in much brighter colours than the saloons, namely:

Exterior	Upholstery
Regency Red	Bright Red with beige piping.
	Bright Green with beige piping.
Shires Green	Bright Green with beige piping.
	Vellum Beige with bright red piping.
Black	Bright Green with beige piping.
	Vellum Beige with bright red piping.
	Bright Red with beige piping.
Clipper Blue	Vellum Beige with bright red piping.
Sequoia Cream	Bright Red with beige piping.
	Vellum Beige with bright red piping.

The YT was produced between 1948 and mid-1950 and the chassis numbers were included in the normal Y-series. Of the 877 YTs built, 874 were official export sales, but 42 cars were delivered in the UK (it is rumoured that towards the end of production a number of the cars were sold direct to the British public). One car which was delivered in the UK was KLU 387, which featured in a touring article, 'Exile in Lakeland', in the July 1, 1949 issue of *The Autocar*; interestingly, KLU 387 is still in existence in the UK today and is in fine condition. However, the factory-built YT lacked the elegance of the open car built by the Swiss coachbuilders Reinbolt & Christé, and indeed, with its hood raised it was somewhat ugly, which may well have accounted for its relatively poor sales performance.

Morris Minor over-riders, very similar to those originally fitted to YTs and YBs, as well as to a small number of YAs, adorn this beautiful red YT, which took part in the famous Bay to Birdwood Run in Australia in 1986.
Pic: C. McManus

Although known as Yellow Lady, this 1950 YT, which has found a home in Florida, is in fact finished in Sequoia Cream/Ivory.
Pic: K.S. Winn

A line-up of proud YT owners at a US Gathering of the Faithful. The car nearest the camera is fitted with non-standard wire wheels.
Pic: G.G. Werbizky

The Y/T/EX(U) lighting arrangements applicable for certain states of the USA called for flashing direction indicators to be fitted to the rear wings.
Pic: G.G. Werbizky

This superbly restored left-hand drive YT belongs to Bernie Havel, of Port Huron, Michigan.
Pic: B. Havel

CHAPTER 4

The YB saloon

Towards the end of 1951, The M.G. Car Company planned a major mechanical update of the YA saloon. The YB, as it was officially called, became available in 1952 and incorporated many of the mechanical advances made in the early postwar years which were by then appearing on other manufacturers' new models.

To begin with, a completely new Lockheed braking system was fitted incorporating a twin leading shoe arrangement on the front wheels and a combined front hub and brake drum (these had been separate components on the YA). This led to significantly increased braking efficiency. Next, a hypoid back axle, based on that fitted to the TD sports car, replaced the old Morris 10 type. A hypoid unit is one in which, as the Nuffield house magazine *Motoring* put it, 'the teeth slide across each other instead of merely delivering the drive with a push'. The hypoid unit thus gave much longer life and quieter running. An 8in diameter clutch appeared in place of the former 7¼in diameter unit.

The YA had been criticized somewhat for a slight tendency to oversteer, and some of the mechanical modifications introduced on the YB sought to remedy this. The wheels were 15in instead of 16in diameter, and a front anti-roll bar was fitted. At the rear there were heavier-duty shock absorbers.

Amongst the electrical equipment, a more modern Lucas RB106 voltage control regulator replaced the RF95 combined fusebox and regulator, and twin windtone horns were fitted, one at each top corner of the engine bay bulkhead.

Bumper over-riders were now made generally available and, as a consequence of the introduction of 15in wheels and wider-section tyres (5.50s instead of the previous 5.00/5.25s), the YB's rear wing panels were deeper directly above the rear wheels and the spare wheel compartment opening and lid became 1in deeper. This difference in rear wing shape can be very hard to judge unless a YA and YB can be examined together. Lastly, when production of the YB began, it was decided that the headlamp backshells would be finished in the same shade of paint as the body of the car, whilst the rims remained chromium-plated. Later, in 1953, the factory reverted to fitting all-chrome headlamps. The main specification changes are tabulated in **Fig 2**. However, as has been stated elsewhere, given the nature of production at Abingdon, there was always the possibility of anomalies to official specifications. YB 0305 was one such; it had all-chrome headlamps!

The owner of an early YB could have been surprised to find that his car did not have all the advertised up-to-date features. The new rear axle, for instance, was not fitted until car number

Nearside engine bay detail of a late YB. One of the car's two Lucas WT614 wind-tone horns can just be seen at the extreme right of the illustration.

Pic: Gary Mills

This pair of pictures clearly illustrates the different profiles of the rear wings of the YA and the YB below it.

Pics: J.G. Lawson

YA meets YB. Here again the differing rear wing profiles are evident, the white car in the background, of course, being the younger YB.

Pic: H.J. Luer

Bodywork differences between the YA and the YB also extend to the size of the spare wheel compartment. The larger compartment of the YB can be seen below right.

Pics: J.G. Lawson & M.J.P. Harris

YB 0286 (the 36th YB off the production line). The new Lucas RB106 voltage control regulator did not appear until YB 0326 (even though it featured in a November 1951 print of the *YA Owners' Handbook*!) and the twin windtone horns were not available until YB 0460 was completed.

In addition, there were many other small differences between the YA and YB, and throughout production of the Y-series small modifications and modernizations were made. Research has also shown that it is difficult to be categorical as regards originality as there were many instances of special equipment being specified by the customer, and these cars retained an element of personalized building, although they were built on a production line and with

Without doubt, one of the best original YBs in Britain, this car, chassis no. YB 1054, belongs to Nicholas Legh-Jones, of Kent.

Pic: P.N. Legh-Jones

YB 0647, owned by David Mullen, of Liverpool, showing the windscreen and sunroof slightly open and the scuttle-mounted radio aerial. Roof-mounted aerials seem to have been more popular, but Y-types had provision for this lower mounting which was much favoured for the T-series sports cars.

Pic: J.G. Lawson

pressed-steel bodies in an attempt, presumably, to standardize and simplify production.

The YB cost £989 including Purchase Tax throughout its production run (which ended in late 1953 after 1,301 cars had been built). As usual, M.G. were hoping for export sales of this revised model. In the event they delivered two bare chassis abroad, 36 'completely knocked down' cars and, as far as can be ascertained, only three fully built YBs, these being earmarked for the directors of P & R Williams Ltd, of Sydney, Australia (authorized M.G. dealers) for the use of their wives. There is no evidence of any left-hand-drive YBs having been built.

YB 1506 is a very original, late 1953 YB finished in Regency Red (Autumn Red) and owned by Barry Bray, from Leyland, Lancashire. Named Demelza, it is fitted with original-type over-riders, which should be compared with the Morris Minor type illustrated on previous pages.

Pic: J.G. Lawson

Several Y-types have acquired prewar 'MG' registration numbers over the years. This is YB 1524, which used to be owned by the author.

Pic: J.G. Lawson

YBs appear to have been available in the following choices of finish:

Exterior	Upholstery
Shires Green	Dark Green with beige piping. Beige with brown piping.
Autumn Red	Dark Red with beige piping. Beige with brown piping.
Black	Dark Red with beige piping. Dark Green with beige piping. Beige with brown piping.
Old English White	Red with beige piping. Beige with brown piping. Dark Green with beige piping.
Silver Streak Grey (a metallic)	Dark Red with beige piping.
Sun Bronze (a metallic)	Dark Red with beige piping. Beige with brown piping.

It should be noted that by this time Shires Green was being referred to as Woodland Green for advertising purposes.

By 1953, the YB's prewar styling was beginning to appear very much out of place alongside the latest 'full-width' unitary construction designs being offered by virtually every manufacturer. However, features such as the sliding roof as a standard fitting were becoming very rare by 1952 and several motoring journalists regretted its passing and were glad that this facility still persisted on the YB. As is the case today, fashion, rather than an appreciation of true craftsmanship, primarily dictated the level of sales, and production of the Y-type in its latest form began to slow. The motoring press of the time well realized this and many articles which appeared about the YB made a point of stressing lamentingly that the YB belonged to

Another car to carry one of the coveted 'MG' registration numbers is this example, chassis no. Y 1505, which underwent a change of wing colour and hub caps between the time these two pictures were taken.

Pics: G.O. Wallis & D.M. Gilbert

By the time YB production was under way, sales brochures were becoming somewhat more colourful, although a certain amount of artistic licence was still evident in the rendition of the car's overall profile!
Pic: J.G. Lawson

another, bygone era. *Motor Industry* magazine, for instance, no doubt influenced by the car's traditional British qualities, said that the YB 'can be classified in the connoisseur category'.

During its best years of production (1949 and 1950), 2,000 Y-types per annum were leaving Abingdon. In 1953, only just over 600 were completed. It was time for M.G. to move with the times and, in 1954, along came the Z-type Magnette, a wholly new design which featured hardly any of the parts used in the construction of its predecessor.

Fig 2   **SERIES YB – SPECIFICATION CHANGES**

From chassis no.	Details of modification.
YB 0286	Front hub and brake drum to true YB specification (twin leading shoe). Hypoid rear axle introduced. New type of wheelbrace included in toolkit.
YB 0326	Voltage control regulator changed from RF95/2 to RB106.
YB 0460	Twin windtone horns, associated equipment and modified wiring loom introduced.
YB 1352	New type of semaphore arms introduced.
YB 1220	New specification for steering ball joint parts.
YB 1240	All-chrome headlamps re-introduced (cars YB 0251 to YB 1239 had chrome rims to headlamps and backshells finished in the same colour as the car body).

NUP 587, chassis no. YB 1184, has its headlamp backshells painted in the car's red body colour, but 55 cars later the factory went back to fitting all-chrome headlamps. MYW 10, an award-winning 1952 YB owned by M.A. Parker, of Leeds, was one of the first Y-types to be restored to concours condition.

Pics: A. Tallentire & M.A. Parker

CHAPTER 5

The XPAG engine

The engine which powers the Y-type saloons and tourers began life, as we have seen in an earlier chapter, as the 1,140cc XPJM unit fitted to the Morris 10 Series M saloon in late 1938. In this guise it had a bore of 63.5mm and a stroke of 90mm and with a compression ratio of 6.6/6.8:1 it gave a maximum power output of 37.2bhp at 4,600rpm. This engine was also fitted to the Wolseley 10 as the XPJW and to the wartime Morris 10 utility car as the XPJM/U (with a Solex instead of an S.U. carburettor).

The 1,250cc bored-out version of the engine (bore 66.5mm, stroke 90mm, compression ratio 7.2/7.4:1), designated XPAG, first appeared in the M.G. TB Midget of 1939 and then, after the war, in the TC. Apart from its use in the Y-series which we will look at here, it was also fitted to the later TD and TF Midgets and, as the XPAW, to the Wolseley 4/44 saloon. Incidentally, the only outward difference between the XPAG and the XPAW engine was that the Wolseley variant had its oil dipstick mounted on the opposite side of the block (the offside) to that of the M.G. unit. Compared with the XPJM, the XPAG had greater rigidity in all moving parts, a stronger block and crankshaft and larger inlet and exhaust valves.

The XPAG engine was a four-cylinder, in-line, overhead-valve (pushrod-operated), water-cooled engine. It employed a cast-iron cylinder head and crankcase, the latter split at $\frac{1}{8}$in below the crankshaft centreline and mated at that point to an aluminium sump of initially 9 and later $10\frac{1}{2}$ pints capacity (the XPJM sump, incidentally, contained only $5\frac{1}{2}$ pints of oil). Compared with a design having a deep block and a pressed-steel sump, the XPAG arrangement had several advantages. The block, while much lighter, had plenty of stiffness in a vertical plane, while the aluminium-alloy sump, which enclosed the bottom half of a cast-iron flywheel on to which the starter ring gear was heat-shrunk, was fixed by studs to the bellhousing. This improved considerably the stiffness of the whole unit, and in particular maintained the alignment of the crankshaft and gearbox drive-shaft. The sump as fitted to Y-types differed from that fitted to earlier XPAG-engined cars (namely the M.G. TB and TC) in that the Y-type unit had had to be modified to accommodate the forward movement of the clutch swivel mechanism. The four-throw crankshaft was carried on three renewable steel shell, white-metalled main bearings which were dowel-located. Thrust was taken by the flanged centre main bearing.

The connecting rod big-end bearings were of the renewable thin steel shell, white-metalled type, whilst the connecting rods were much strengthened from those of the original XPJM unit. Strengthening modifications continued to be made to the connecting rods throughout

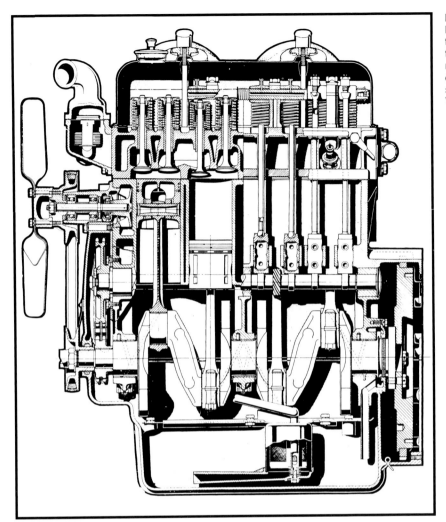

Longitudinal section of the M.G. XPAG engine which the Y-type saloons and tourers shared, with only minor variations in specification, with the T-series sports cars as well as the Wolseley 4/44 saloon.

the production run of the XPAG engine. The oval-skirted pistons were made from Aerolite aluminium alloy and each was fitted with two compression rings and one slotted scraper ring. Gudgeon pins were a push fit and were secured by clamp bolts.

The three-bearing camshaft was driven from the crankshaft by duplex roller chain. The gear-type oil pump was externally spigotted into the nearside of the crankcase (its external mounting aiding in the cooling of the oil) and was driven from the camshaft. It supplied a full-flow oil filter. Fuel was supplied by an electrically-operated S.U. pump to a single (in the case of the saloons) and twin (in the case of the YT) semi-downdraught, variable-venturi S.U. carburettor(s). A 12-volt ignition system was fitted, the distributor being driven by the camshaft and fitted to the nearside of the block.

The silchrome steel valves were slightly inclined in the cylinder head, the inlet valves being of 30mm and the exhaust valves 26mm diameter; double valve springs were employed. The inlet and exhaust manifolds were cast integrally.

The engine was mounted to the chassis by a central rubber-bonded sandwich at the front and, at the rear, the gearbox rested on two loose rubber blocks in a frame cradle and was located by a single central drawbolt pin-jointed to the gearbox to allow for oscillation of the power unit. Additionally, there was a transverse torque reaction link at the front of the engine, mounted near the top right-hand side of the block and fastened to the frame to give the power

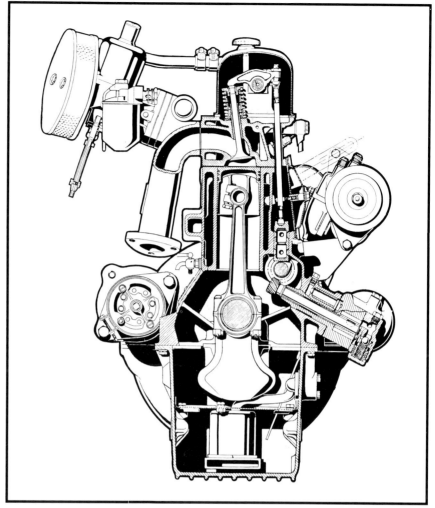

A transverse section of the same engine. The XPAG power units were the subject of an ongoing programme of development and refinement throughout the production life of the Y-type cars.

unit lateral stability at its upper extremities.

The offside of the engine carried the carburettor(s), fuel pump, starter motor and intake and exhaust manifolds, whilst on the nearside were the spark plugs, distributor, oil pump and filter and dynamo. This neat and functional separation of the ignition and fuel systems was to become a feature of BMC engine design in the late forties and into the fifties when those two great mainstays of BMC, and later British Leyland, the A and B-series engines, appeared.

Two separately-designated variants of the XPAG engine were fitted to Y-type M.G.s: XPAG/SC/10001 to 16915 (the number was usually prefixed by an X when the car was for export) and XPAG/SC2/16916 to 18460. The SC2 version of the engine was not introduced with the first YB, as is often assumed to have been the case, but was first fitted to a batch of late 1951 Ys. Engines intended for YTs (these were fitted with twin carburettors) were numbered XPAG/TR for RHD cars and XPAG/TL for LHD cars.

Usually, engines fitted to export cars had the letter X as a prefix to the five-figure serial number. It has been confirmed, however, that not all export engines were so designated and the addition of the X may have been determined by whether or not an export (or tropical) air filter was fitted.

Development of the engine continued throughout its life from 1938 to 1954 in the never-ending quest for more power and improved torque at low speeds. The table reproduced at

These photographs, taken in 1946, are of an early XPAG/SC engine. The ornate chrome rocker box cover and fittings were presumably for display purposes and certainly did not appear on production examples.
Pics: The British Motor Industry Heritage Trust – Austin Rover Group

Fig 3 outlines the major changes which took place in the specification of engines fitted in Y-type M.G.s, but it will be noted that reference is made to *three* distinct groupings of these engines.

In 1952, a major redesign of the block and cylinder head was made to improve cooling and breathing. Later engines can conveniently be referred to as Group 3 engines and it should be noted that blocks, cylinder heads and associated gaskets from Group 3 engines are not interchangeable with items from engines within Groups 1 and 2. It must also be emphasized that so-called Group 3 engines were not separately designated on their cars' documentation or identification plates.

A neat Shorrocks super-charger installation on a 1948 YA.
Pic: Tory Skopecek

The cooling system of this engine deserves special mention as its design is primarily responsible for the 'tunability' of the engine. The block ran warmer than the head. Water was directed particularly to the cylinder head where there were more than adequate water passages. The flow was therefore almost entirely channelled through the cylinder head. The block received mostly static water and therefore ran at a slightly higher temperature.

All nuts and bolts used in the assembly of the XPAG engine have metric threads, although they retain Whitworth flats. Furthermore, the threads differ from the ISO metric specification used today. This unusual situation came about in 1919, when all Morris engines were manufactured by the French firm of Hotchkiss at their Coventry factory. Naturally, the U.K. factory adopted the metric taps and dies of its French parent.

M.G., of course, had an illustrious racing and competition history and for many years before the Second World War had co-operated actively with owners' requests for tuning information and components. The TC sports car had not long been in production before Abingdon acceded to the constant demands for information on tuning the XPAG engine and, in 1949, a booklet entitled *Special Tuning for the M.G. Midget Engine* was produced. This publication gave details of five separate stages of factory-backed and approved tuning. The factory would undertake to do the work required by a prospective owner when time permitted (it was explained that at that time M.G. were working flat-out to fill large export orders) or components could be supplied so that the owner could do the work himself.

In addition to this comprehensive programme of tuning the basic engine, a number of supercharger manufacturers also supplied units which were approved by Abingdon as compatible with the XPAG engine. The four different types of supercharger came from Shorrock, Marshall-NORDEC, Wade and Arnott. Over 200mph was eventually to be achieved using an XPAG engine in M.G.'s EX.135 record car at the Bonneville Salt Flats in Utah, USA.

Fig 3 **XPAG ENGINE – SPECIFICATION CHANGES**

From engine no.	Details of modification
XPAG/SC/13404	New design of cylinder block guide for dipstick.
14023	Dynamo changed to C45Y-V3 type. Starter changed to M418G type. New type of flywheel ring gear (120 teeth) and starter pinion (12 teeth). Previous ring gear had 93 teeth.
14083	New type of oil pump introduced plus associated equipment (pipe from pump to filter, etc).
15405	Oil filter strap introduced.

15499	Top and third gear sliding hub with cone redesigned.
15576	TD-type pistons introduced.
15926	Suppressor introduced into starter switch circuit.
16431	Top and third gear sliding hub with cone redesigned for second time.
16463	New type of water pump introduced.
16729	Oil pick-up moved to centre of sump.
16769	Dynamo changed to C39 PV-2 type.
16831	Low-overlap (12 thou) camshaft fitted. Cam lift and timing altered. Rocker shaft, plugs and spacer springs modified. New design rockers fitted to nos. 1, 4, 5 and 8 valves.
XPAG/SC2/16916	First Group 2 engine. 8in clutch and different type of flywheel fitted.
17020	Shorter dipstick and guide tube fitted.
17293	Cylinder block redesigned. Integral oil pump and filter introduced. Oil filter bypass spring and ball ceased with engine no. 17292.
17383	Larger capacity sump introduced (10½ pints) including a baffle plate. Suction filter assembly introduced.
17432	Shorter pushrods introduced, along with longer adjusting screws. Speedometer gear key introduced in gearbox.
17463	Further cylinder block redesign. First Group 3 engine. Employed longer-reach spark plugs and different gaskets for improved cooling.
17670	Priming plug fitted to oil pump. Distributor clamp parts redesigned.
17994	New-design cylinder head gasket along with further change in type of spark plugs.
18097	New-type cylinder head cover. New-design camshaft fitted (19 thou). Distributor type 40058F introduced. Suction filter assembly redesigned again.
18120	Oil pump again redesigned.
18122	Yet another type of spark plug introduced.
18272	Crankshaft redesign.

Summary:

Group 1 engines:	SC/10001 to 16915
Group 2 engines:	SC2/16916 to 17462
Group 3 engines:	SC2/17463 to 18460

CHAPTER 6

Y-types in competition

The Y-type, of course, was never designed to be a competitive sports car but, nevertheless, it had its moments with those drivers whose preference was racing or rallying saloon cars. And it was particularly useful and popular at 'club' level.

After the Second World War, motor sport took some while to regain its feet. Italy, however, was relatively quick off the mark and re-introduced the famous 1,000-mile road race, the Mille Miglia, in 1947. *The Autocar* magazine sent John Dugdale and another staff member with a brand-new Y-type, provided by the factory and registered DRX 557, to cover the event.

In the British public's eye, the Monte Carlo Rally was the major European rallying event. Before the war, cars had started from points all over Europe to finish in that most attractive and affluent area of the Mediterranean. No doubt the glamour and wealth associated with Monte Carlo accounted in part for the public's interest in this event. To seasoned rally drivers, however, the 'Monte', whilst attracting a great deal of welcome publicity, was never the most demanding, nor the most rewarding rally. There was no Monte Carlo Rally after the war until 1949. On that occasion, Glasgow was the only British starting point and the average journey which entrants, from whatever starting point, had to make to reach Monte Carlo was 1,955 miles. In 1950, an extreme winter, only five cars made it to Monte Carlo without penalty. That year, OWL 543, an Almond Green YA, was entered for the rally, driven by experienced rally and racing driver Betty Haig with Barbara Marshall as co-driver. One year later, Major and Mrs A. Pownall entered their Y-type in the rally and made it to Monte Carlo, coming 45th in the final test.

Meanwhile, on the UK domestic scene, that other prestigious event, the RAC Rally, had been reinstated, and in the 1951 event Y-types were successful in the under-1,500cc closed cars class. First in class was J. Readings with J. Shaw third. Further down the field, Mrs L.E. Grounds, in 23rd place, is thought to have driven a Y, and another competitor in a 'Y' was F.M. Baker.

The 1951 1,000-mile Circuit of Ireland Trial saw at least five Y-types competing, known drivers being J.M. McCaughan, R.J. Caldwell, J.E. McGrath, D.A. Wilkins and Mrs J.J. Flynn, Mrs Flynn winning the Ladies' Trophy, and in 1954 Dr E.S. Dorman drove Y-type OZ 5708 in the same event. Another famous lady rally driver of the time was Lady Samuelson, who is known to have owned a 1950 YA (registration number LPO 900), but there is no record of it having been entered for any competitive events.

In 1953, three specially-built and prepared YBs (HMO 908, 909 and 910) were entered for the

RAC Rally, and were crewed by R.E. Holt, J.L. Shaw and G.R. Holt. At the end of that season Len Shaw bought HMO 909 from the manufacturers and retains it, in rally trim, to this day. He and the car came sixth in the general category and won class and team prizes in the 1953 rally. More recently, the car took part in the commemorative RAC Golden Fifty Rally in 1982, again driven by Len Shaw.

After it had competed in the 1950 Monte Carlo Rally, OWL 543 was sold to Shaw by John Thornley, then the general manager of M.G., and it raced and rallied quite successfully. The names Shaw, Readings, Baker and Grant (referred to later) appear again and again in reports of competitive events during the early fifties, and on many of these occasions these gentlemen drove Y-type M.G.s. Regrettably, HMO 908, HMO 910 and OWL 543 have all since been scrapped.

One name which is very much associated with M.G. in competitive events, and particularly with Y-types, is that of Dick Jacobs. It was he whom John Thornley credits as being the driving force in the early fifties in persuading M.G. to re-enter motor sport, albeit semi-officially to begin with. Dick Jacobs' first involvement with Y-types came in 1950 when he approached John Thornley with a view to acquiring a competitive M.G. for the coming 1951 season. The result of this approach was that the development shop at Abingdon built him a special chassis equipped with Y-type independent front suspension (apparently the Y-type's front suspension components were lighter than those fitted to the TD sports car, notwithstanding the fact that the two systems were in all other important respects identical). The chassis, registered SHK 7, was delivered in December 1950 and Jacobs and Ken Keemer, who was chargehand at his Mill Garage in South Woodford, Essex, built a light aluminium body on to it. They also used an XPAG engine with a short-stroke Laystall crankshaft which gave the engine a capacity of 1,088cc.

Perhaps the most illustrious competition performances in a Y-type, however, were Dick Jacobs' three wins in consecutive years (1952, 1953 and 1954) in his YB, chassis number YB 0414, registered UHK 111, at Silverstone in the BRDC Production Touring Car races sponsored by the *Daily Express*. Jacobs had wanted to race one of the new YBs so, early in 1952, he wrote to the Nuffield sales manager, Tom Sangster, for help. On April 14, the maroon YB was delivered – Jacobs had just three weeks to run it in and prepare it for its first race. Testing took place each night until 600 miles had been accomplished. The valves were then ground in, 150lb valve springs were fitted and the carburettor choke size was increased. Apart from those modifications, the car remained in standard production specification for the first year *and* it was driven to and from the circuit.

In the 17-lap race, the YB constantly diced with three Jowett Javelins and eventually won Class F (1,100 to 1,500cc). Next year, performance was improved slightly to cope with opposition from a very fast side-valve Morris Minor, an Austin A40, a Riley, a Simca, three Jowett Javelins and another YB, UMG 662, owned by Gregor Grant, the editor of *Autosport*, and driven by George Phillips. Again UHK 111 won the class, with UMG 662 third.

For 1954, Dick Jacobs had hoped to drive one of the new M.G. ZA Magnettes at the *Daily Express* Silverstone meeting in May. However, due to production delays this was not to be and the old faithful UHK 111 was brought out of retirement. Changes in regulations now permitted almost any engine modification providing the bore and stroke remained unaltered. Thus, in line with current Abingdon development shop practice, Martlett pistons with raised crowns were used, which gave a higher compression ratio. An XPEG camshaft was installed, but the TD Mark II manifold with twin 1½in S.U. carburettors was retained initially. Again the car was run in at night, this time over a distance of 1,000 miles. Peak performance achieved by these modifications was 88mph at 6,100rpm in top gear. Fitting an XPEG manifold together with twin 1¾in S.U.s increased the top speed to 95mph and the maximum revs to 6,900rpm in third gear. These performance increases had been necessitated by potential opposition

A famous car and evidence of its successes. This is the illustrious UHK 111, the YB which won its class in the Production Touring Car races at Silverstone in 1952, 1953 and 1954 in the hands of Dick Jacobs.
Pic: Alan White

UHK III
1500 cc CLASS WINNER.
B.R.D.C. SILVERSTONE
PRODUCTION TOURING CAR RACE
MAY 10TH. 1952.

AND
MAY 9TH 1953.

AND AGAIN
MAY 15TH 1954

SUPPLIED BY
MILL GARAGE
E.18.

from a Borgward but, despite this, the YB again went on to win its class, for the third year running. UHK 111 still exists today, in Kent, and is in fine condition.

Dick Jacobs also received the last YB chassis off the production line (numbered YB 1551) and on this he and Ken Keemer built a glassfibre full-width coupé body. The car, initially registered XNO 1, was given a 1,500cc engine and Wolseley 6/80 front brakes. Knock-off TD wire wheels were also employed. The one competitive success of this car in Jacobs' hands was at a 1-kilometre straight sprint at the USAF base at Wethersfield, in Essex, on July 4, 1954. It won its class together with an award for being the fastest M.G. on the day. More recently the car was re-registered 982 VWL and is known to have been raced at Snetterton. It was last heard of in 1979, so it may still exist.

A competitive achievement of a different sort was accomplished by the well-known record-breaker Goldie Gardner in Belgium in July 1950. An M.G. distributor from Brighton by the name of Richard Benn believed that the Y-type might be able to achieve 100mph if it was appropriately tuned. He thus set about having his car tuned to Stage V with the aid of Syd Enever and Reg 'Jacko' Jackson from the Abingdon factory. Included amongst the tuning modifications was a Shorrocks supercharger giving 6½lb of boost, the underneath of the car was improved aerodynamically and oversize rear tyres were fitted. It was then taken to the Jabbeke highway in Belgium where Major Gardner made several runs, the best of which recorded a speed of 107.36mph. The average came out at 104.725mph for the flying mile and 104.713mph for the 5-kilometre distance, all these speeds being officially timed and verified.

In relating this story I feel I must put the record straight as regards the state of the car after the several high-speed runs had been made. There is a recurrent myth in M.G. circles that after the runs the car's engine blew up, or 'made loud noises', and the story has been repeated again and again in publications on the M.G. marque. However, to clarify matters, I quote from the article on the subject written by Russell Lowry, which appeared in *Motoring* magazine, the house magazine of the Nuffield Organisation: 'Then, having satisfied his own quiet, unshaken argument, Richard Benn stepped into his closed carriage and motored himself sedately home to Brighton . . .'.

Although not strictly competitive, Sidney J. Perelman's journey from Paris to Peking in his YT in 1978 deserves a mention here. The idea initially was for *The Sunday Times* to publish a series of articles written by the American humourist and traveller recounting his journey. The black YT had been bought by Perelman in Bangkok in 1949 and for a long time had been stored in the premises of a bankrupt delicatessen in Philadelphia. Before beginning its epic trip to Peking it had only covered 19,000 miles in the intervening 29 years. British Leyland donated a Land Rover to accompany the YT and two other M.G. enthusiasts went along to look after the car's needs, taking with them a large quantity of spares. Perelman and the car made it to Peking (via France, Italy, Yugoslavia, Bulgaria, Turkey, Iran, India, Burma and Hong Kong) although sadly, once the trip was over, he became ill and, nine months later, passed away. His observations on the trip, alas, were never published. It is worth noting in conclusion, as symptomatic of the world in which we live today, that by the time the YT reached Peking all its M.G. badges had disappeared, stolen by souvenir-hunters.

In more recent years, Frank Vautier became notable for his spirited performances in what started life as a 1951 Sun Bronze YA. This car was extensively modified with advice from Dick Jacobs during its long competitive life (it still occasionally appears at 'club' events today). Among the modifications carried out were the fitting of larger twin S.U. carburettors, a ZA Magnette rear axle, two front anti-roll bars, MGA disc brakes at the front, radial tyres and, eventually, a supercharger. Then, one day in the summer of 1974, at Wiscombe Park Hillclimb, Devon, the car was modified in quite a different way when it was rolled on to its roof while taking a hairpin a little too fast. Once the car was righted, the driver took up his position behind the wheel and the Y-type was able to continue to the top of the hill!

CHAPTER 7

Y-type special bodies

Before the Second World War all but a very few types of car employed a separate strongly built chassis on to which a body was bolted. The body was invariably either coachbuilt, that is to say it was constructed by having metal panels fixed to a wooden framework or, towards the end of the thirties, it was of pressed-steel construction. It was therefore comparatively easy, given this method of construction, for different types of body other than those offered by the manufacturers to be fitted to chassis. Indeed, coachbuilding businesses which did just this abounded, and the variety of special-bodied derivatives of both mass-produced and more up-market cars of the period was very significant. After the war, however, as the unitary construction method of car production began to take the place of the more traditional methods, the opportunities for these once renowned coachbuilders steadily declined and today it is virtually impossible to rebody a factory-produced car to one's liking or design.

The Y-type M.G., however, as we have seen, was basically a prewar design and employed a separate chassis on to which was bolted a pressed-steel body. Thus, production had not been underway for long before coachbuilders began to look at the car with a view to offering different body styles for different markets, as had been the case with prewar M.G.s

One of the more noteworthy coachbuilding firms .who had carried out very elegant rebodying work on a number of prewar M.G. SA saloons was Reinbolt & Christé S.A., of Basle, in Switzerland. Mr Emil Frey imported three early 1948 YA chassis and Reinbolt & Christé gave them very distinctive two-door convertible bodywork, the three cars appearing with dark blue, maroon and dark green paintwork, respectively, and all three having beige upholstery. It should be remembered that the factory-produced YT convertible was not available until the autumn of that year. It is certainly this author's view that the Reinbolt & Christé convertible (which has since been referred to unofficially as the YRC) is by far the neater and more handsome of the two convertible offerings.

An article in *The Autocar* for May 14, 1948 suggests that there were to be Zagato-bodied Ys for the US market. Apparently, this design exercise was undertaken by the Italian coachbuilders at the behest of Mr Roger Barlow, President of International Motors, of Los Angeles. Open two-seaters and drophead two- and four-seaters were to be built. Neither were the changes to be limited to the provision of a different style of bodywork, for Zagato had plans to make one or two modifications to the chassis, engine specification and instruments. There were plans to produce up to 70 of these cars with bodywork by Zagato, Castagna and Farina, but evidence has only come to light of one, with coupé bodywork by Zagato, having actually been produced and it is not known whether this was released to the public. Indeed, the Abingdon works export statistics seem to suggest that this project never really progressed beyond the prototype stage because only 11 'chassis only' are listed as having been delivered, nine in 1948 (three of which would be the YRCs referred to above) and one each in 1952 and 1953.

Not so much a special body, but more a modified standard saloon, was the car prepared by University Coachwork Ltd for an American customer in 1951. The rear quarter lights were blanked off and in their place were fitted dummy hood irons to give the impression of a drop-head arrangement. Covers were also fitted over the rear wheels, increasing the depth of the rear wings to a point where only the hubcaps of the wheels were visible. Flashing trafficators were fitted to comply with the latest US lighting regulations and the bumpers were raised and the fixing points strengthened, the bumper blades being fitted with large TD-type over-riders.

In the previous chapter, mention was made of the special coupé body built on the last YB chassis made, YB 1551. This car was prepared specially for racing by Dick Jacobs and was initially registered XNO 1. Its very modern full-width bodywork was a whole generation in motor car bodywork design ahead of the standard factory offering (which, it should be remembered, was designed in the late thirties).

Undoubtedly, several more special-bodied Y-types must have been prepared whilst the car was still in production. One example which has come to light appeared in the 'cars for sale' columns of *The Autocar* of March 4, 1949. It is described as follows: 'Tankard & Smith Ltd. offer M.G. 1¼-Litre fitted with very attractive and special 2-door saloon in black with beige leather upholstery and black carpets, many extras including windscreen spray, exterior and interior as new, mechanically 100%, moderate mileage; £735; 3 months' written guarantee . . . . 198 Kings Road, S.W.3. . . .'

At the risk of offending the so-called 'purists', it might even be said that the famous M.G. TD sports car started life as a special-bodied Y-type. Works manager Cecil Cousins recounted some years ago how at Abingdon they took a Y-type chassis and cut 5in out of the centre of the frame and put a sleeve up inside it. Then a TC body was placed on the chassis, various modifications were made and in about three weeks the TD was born.

Since the days when the Y-type was in production many private individuals have probably had a go at fitting their own specially designed bodies to the Y-type chassis. After all, it was of quite advanced design when it appeared in 1947 and gave good handling coupled with excellent rigidity and durability. By the time the sixties and early seventies arrived there were a great number of neglected Y-type saloons around which could be acquired very cheaply indeed and thus they lent themselves to conversion or rebodying by those whose interest lay in that direction.

One rebodied car which came to light a few years ago in Gloucestershire was NTV 298. This had been given a glassfibre low-slung sports coupé body with rectangular headlights and was fitted with an XPEG engine taken from a TF 1500. No further details of this car's history are known.

In Australia, it seems that there is a 1947 YA which during its life has acquired a YT body, while in Holland there is perhaps the most ambitious rebodying project of all; an enterprising owner has built on to the back of a cut-off saloon body, which had suffered an accident, a tow-truck flat bed complete with towing crane!

Lastly, there are the TF replicas, at least three of which are known to exist. Given what was said above about the way in which the TD was developed, and bearing in mind that nowadays many people would like to own a T-type but are unable to afford the high prices which genuine examples command, it is not surprising that several of these 'conversions' have appeared. Unfortunately, back in 1979, at least one of these Y-type chassis with a TF body was being passed off by a car dealer as a genuine TF. So, beware!

This 1948 Y-type chassis with special convertible bodywork by Reinbolt & Christé S.A. is owned by Ernst Kengelbacher, of Leichtenstein. Hood up or down, it has a style which many feel was lacking in the factory-produced YT. Note that the windscreen wipers are scuttle-mounted, whereas on the YT they are mounted on the windscreen frame.

Pics: E. Kengelbacher

CHAPTER 8

Buyer's guide

There was a period during the sixties, the seventies and into the early eighties when many Y-types were available to the prospective buyer very cheaply indeed. Stories are common of owners acquiring their cars for little or even no outlay whatever. Serious concours restoration of Y-types is only a recent phenomenon, and values did not begin to increase to any great extent until 1982 or so. Even genuine low-mileage cars in original condition did not command very high prices. Nowdays, however, the choice of cars on offer at any one time has become much more limited as a direct result of the growing acceptance of the Y-type as a car worth owning, restoring and preserving.

When contemplating ownership it is now possible to choose between the dismantled, abandoned restoration, the roadworthy but unrestored car, the genuine low-mileage, original example, or the already restored 'concours' vehicle. Much of the advice appearing in this chapter is concerned with the possible problem areas which will be found on an unrestored car. It must be said here, though, that if you are considering buying a dismantled or partly dismantled example it will be very difficult indeed to ensure that all the components necessary to make up a complete car are included in the purchase.

Remember that although many mechanical, engine and trim parts are available from the various suppliers mentioned in the following chapter, some items are very difficult to find and may only be obtainable by locating a secondhand original example. Such secondhand parts are much more difficult to obtain today than they were, say, five years ago. Many owners have at least one spare car in poor condition which they have had to buy in order to obtain some missing and fairly rare part. Remember also that new reproduction items can be fairly expensive (the magic of the M.G. name which ensures their availability can also result in high prices being asked) and may not always be of a quality and fit equal to the original part.

It is assumed in what follows that the reader is familiar with all the general advice regarding points to be borne in mind and tests to be carried out when purchasing a used car. Such advice often appears in the glossy monthly motoring magazines. You should apply your knowledge as much to a Y-type as to any more modern car, with the following additions and modifications.

Chassis

The major diffference between a Y-type and most modern cars is that the Y has a sizeable and

Let's hope they were cheap! Three examples of how a Y-type may look when you see a prospective purchase for the first time. But do not despair – there are probably even more daunting examples elsewhere. The one-headlamp car, below left, was photographed in Sydney, Australia, in May 1982.

Pics: A.Taylor & P. Holsgrove

sturdy chassis on to which the engine, body and running gear are bolted. The chassis will rarely be found to exhibit severe corrosion. If it does, then go no further; you'd be better off looking at some other Ys. The only place on the chassis where a measure of corrosion is sometimes found is where the chassis passes under the back axle. Here, water, mud and salt drip down, with the predictable result. Most Ys are not severely corroded here and a spot of welding will usually cure the problem.

Under this heading, too, comes accident damage. If the accident has been a bad one and the chassis frame is severely distorted then, here again, it is best to look elsewhere. You will see many Ys with bumpers and headlamp bars not parallel and with wings and front valances somewhat misaligned. This may indicate that there has been some misalignment of the chassis frame due to an accident. Usually, minor misalignment is no problem; it rarely seems to affect steering and suspension efficiency.

Bodywork

You will no doubt find corrosion in the following areas to some extent: The bottom third or so of all four doors; the box sections behind the running boards and the bottoms of the central door pillars (the box sections are not, of course, 'structural' on a Y and unless corrosion is very severe this should not be an MOT failure area); the rear wheelarches where the wings bolt on to the body (it is often very hard to tell the extent of the corrosion here from a simple external examination – do not be fooled by a car which looks good because unless it has been rebuilt properly corrosion will usually be present!); floors of the spare wheel compartment and boot and adjoining areas; spare wheel compartment lid and lower part of bootlid.

Repair panels are often available in respect of all the above areas, but supplies can be intermittent. Check for full and free operation of the sunroof and for corrosion around the drainage hoses (if possible) where they disappear inside the headlining.

Mechanical components

One of the most often-repeated legends (one might even say myths) concerning the YA and YT is that the rear axle half-shafts break very easily. Stories abound of owners making it a rule never to leave home in their Ys without taking along a spare half-shaft in the spare wheel compartment (often alongside that spare S.U. fuel pump, which American owners in particular seem to have problems with)!

It is true that the half-shafts fitted to the YA/YT rear axle are not the most robust in the world and they will break if they have had a history of rough treatment such as from attempts to be quick off the line at traffic lights (in a 'Y'?) or prolonged competitive use at 'club' level, for instance). However, in the author's view, half-shaft breakage is not and never has been a major problem. By all means acquire a spare or two if you can (and it is possible to change one at the roadside if you really have to) but be careful, if you acquire secondhand half-shafts, to ensure that you know from which side of the donor car they have been removed and make sure you fit them to the same side in your car, otherwise you will increase the chance of a further breakage. YA/YT half-shafts should at all times be treated with respect and newly fitted ones should be run in over several thousand miles. If the half-shafts are removed for any reason, make sure that they are refitted not only to the same side of the car, but that they are relocated in the original spline position.

One of the fascinations of car restoration is the challenge it offers! The dented front wing, above left, gives a new meaning to the term panel-bashing, while the restorer of the car on the right has wisely applied the cutter to remove a badly rotted spare wheel compartment lid and surrounding area.

Pics: P. Holsgrove & A. Taylor

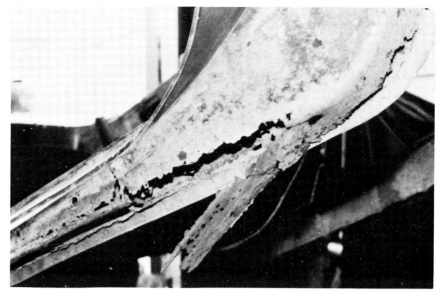

Cars can rust, even around Melbourne, Australia. The corrosion in this YT is typical of that likely to be found in Y-type sills.
Pic: D. Ardill

The Jackall System always provides amusement and amazement to the passing onlooker or the uninitiated observer. You should find that the front arms remain fairly well lubricated by oil leaks from the engine and therefore usually extend and retract very well, whereas the rear arms will have suffered from being covered in road dirt, mud and salt-impregnated slush, and therefore tend to stick in the 'down' position when asked to retract or, at the very least, do not retract properly. Often, rear jacking arms have been bent by fouling driveways or ramps, the driver being ignorant of the fact that one or both of the arms had not retracted properly. It may be necessary to lever the rear arms back to the 'up' positon using a hydraulic jack handle or wheelbrace each time the rear arms are used.

Miles Harris, from Northern Ireland, looks delighted with his purchase of this YB in May 1986.
Pic: M.J.P. Harris

Never get underneath the car when it is supported solely on the Jackall System jacks. They should be used in emergencies only when, for instance, changing a punctured tyre. This is what it was designed for and, whilst it has been shown that the car can remain off the ground on the Jackall arms for a significant length of time, it only needs the presence of one or two air bubbles in the system to bring the car down to earth fairly rapidly.

It may be found that on using the operating handle nothing appears to be happening for some time; do not despair, keep going and eventually (provided the system is in good order) the front or the rear or the whole car as desired will raise itself slowly off the ground. And do make sure that the jacks are operated on a firm, smooth surface; the author once had an embarrassing experience when operating the Jackall System on what turned out to be softish ashphalt. The arms slowly sunk into the ashphalt, leaving the Y-type still firmly grounded!

There exists some confusion over what type of hydraulic fluid to use nowadays in the Jackall System. New owners may quite rightly be wary of disobeying the system instructions to the effect that only Red Jackall Fluid must be used. Worry not; it is true that prewar Jackall Systems were very particular over what fluid was used. Only Green Jackall Fluid must be used in prewar systems as the rubber seals in the jacking arms are made of a compound which will be damaged should any other type of fluid be used. The postwar systems, however, use rubber seals which are much more tolerant and thus any good shock absorber fluid or motorcycle front fork oil should work well in the Y-type's Jackall System.

One of the major improvements embodied in the YB was (as has been referred to elsewhere) the more up-to-date braking system, replacing what was essentially the prewar system of the YA. Thus, at the time of writing, it is still fairly easy to obtain all the components of the YB braking system and, given the fact that the YB's front drum brakes employ twin leading shoes, it can be assumed that the YB's system should provide more efficient stopping power than that afforded by the YA (or YT).

For many years now it has been significantly more difficult to obtain YA brake components. Master cylinders are particularly difficult to find, as are wheel cylinders. Repair kits for master cylinders are still obtainable due, apparently, to the fact that they are still kept in stock for use on various types of commercial vehicles. Wheel cylinder repair kits can be hard to obtain and it goes without saying that, when supplies of these scarce components do occasionally surface, they tend to be quite expensive. Nevertheless, the above said, there are probably four times as many YAs and YTs on the roads than YBs (because of the relative scarcity of YBs due to the much lower production total) so the antiquated nature of the YA's braking system does not seem at the present time to be causing insoluable problems for owners. Master and wheel cylinders can also be overhauled and resleeved by the appropriate specialists.

Interior tirm

Leather upholstery can be very durable and it will often be found that most of the interior will be no more than badly worn with the occasional crack in the seat coverings. Inevitably, the driver's seat always seems to have suffered the most, and here you may even find that the seat has collapsed completely and that the leather is badly torn and damaged. Where only cracking is evident it will usually be possible to restore the leather to an acceptable condition by using one of the proprietary leather renovating kits. Where, however, upholstery is very badly damaged or has disintegrated completely (for instance, when the car has been stored outside and open to the weather) the high cost of restoring leather interiors should be borne in mind (unless some element of non-originality in materials is acceptable).

Finally, a word about headlinings. All headlinings were beige in colour, and although you may find saloons which appear to have black or dark green headlinings, this discolouration will have come about through heavy smoking by previous owners!

You don't find many as bad as this one! However, despite the tree growing through it, this Y-type yielded many useful parts according to its purchaser.

Pic: R. Jesson

Engine

XPAG engines are durable, tough and usually very long-lived. There are several Y-types on the road today which have accomplished more than 300,000 miles on their original engines. Most engine components are readily available from the specialists mentioned in the chapter which follows. Engine components, however, as well as spare engines when they turn up, do tend to be quite expensive. There is a lot of room in the Y-type engine compartment and the engine itself is easy to work on.

Oil leakage from the rear crankshaft oil seal was always a problem, even straight from the factory. Once the engine has warmed up check on this. A small amount of leakage is acceptable, but steer clear of a car which is depositing large pools of oil on the ground! The lack of oil pressure caused by such extensive leakage will be evident by a glance at the oil pressure gauge when the engine is at idle. Pressure at idle should be between 40 and 45psi, and if it is substantially less than this, further prolonged running without remedial action will result in further engine wear and damage.

Present-day operation

Nowadays it may be said that the Y-type, given its poor accceleration in modern traffic, is only really at home on quiet country roads (in other words, like those for which it was primarily designed in the first place). Its relatively low compression ratio makes it happy to run on 2-star petrol and 25mpg should be easily achieved. It is worth keeping the petrol tank topped up as often, out of sight, the flexible tubing which leads down into the petrol inside the tank will have rotted over the years, thus causing fuel pick-up problems if the tank is less than around half-full! If you have only driven modern cars before coming to the Y-type, the following remarks may be of help.

Although the YB's braking system was a whole generation ahead of that of the YA, it is still neccessary (even when the system has been renewed throughout) to virtually stand on the brake pedal in order to stop the car in the distance you would expect from a modern car. So, leave a bigger gap in traffic. The Y-type is slow to accelerate and hard to stop by modern standards, so make allowances for this, even if impatient and discourteous drivers of modern cars do not. Often they will be so surprised to see a Y-type in their mirrors they will almost drive into the car in front anyway!

Changing gear must be done a lot more slowly than in a modern car. The gearbox is, as is repeated again and again in contemporary road tests, positive and a delight, but there must be a definite pause before going down into third from top and even more so when changing down into second. If not, you will continue to crash the gears! Double-declutching, once practised *de rigeur* when Y-types were new, is something which one should try to master. Gearbox rattle is something of which the factory was aware during production, but little can be done about this. However, it is not harmful in any way to the components, and in any case, not all cars seem to suffer.

One feature of the Y's road behaviour which might initially surprise is its precise handling and cornering. Indeed, the Y-type handles far better than many more modern cars. It goes just where it is pointed, and it is only when this aspect of the car is fully appreciated that one comes to understand why M.G. gained such a well-deserved reputation for their handling and cornering ability – a tribute to their Issigonis-inspired coil-sprung front suspension and rack-and-pinion steering. One can see why these systems survived barely unaltered and were fitted to many BMC and BL products right through until the demise of the MGB in 1980. The turning circle of the Y-type is quite adequate and, again, is better than on many more modern cars. The view to the rear is also good, making the car very easy to reverse and park.

If it is one's intention to operate a Y-type all the year round, the only addition which will be of real benefit is an efficient heater. Nowdays, it is hard to imagine how the motoring public of the forties and fifties managed to drive their cars throughout the year without heaters! Some Ys, of course, were fitted with Smiths heaters as optional extras and, no doubt, if the entire system is properly overhauled, this original type of heater may be found to supply adequate warmth. However, as a single concession to present-day technology, it should be possible to fit a very efficient heater in place of the original type.

We are, perhaps, fortunate that Y-types, having all been built before June 30, 1964, do not have to have seat belts fitted, for the design of the bodywork makes it very difficult to fit the normal type adequately. The upper mounting point (that is, the one behind the driver's right shoulder) constitutes the problem. The position of the semaphore arm opening and fittings in the central body pillar make it virtually impossible for a seat belt anchorage to be fitted where it should be and, furthermore, if a bracket were to be correctly welded in place here, the position of the front seats when well back on their runners means that the belt would have little restraining effect as the position of the driver's or passenger's chest is directly opposite or even behind the line of the central body pillar on to which both front and rear doors are hung.

When seat belts became available in the early sixties, the major manufacturer, Kangol, was aware that the design of many older cars presented this problem to owners who wished to fit belts. Thus, they introduced their belt type LD2, which was anchored to two places on the floor of the car and looped up and over the back of the seat, over the shoulder and back across the lap. This type of belt would be ideal for use in a Y. Alas, belt type LD2 is no longer available, so Kangol (or ASE [UK] Ltd, as they are today) recommended the fitting of a three-point competition rally harness type FH101.

CHAPTER 9

Clubs, specialists and books

Clubs

For almost as long as M.G. existed as a manufacturer of motor cars there has been at least one club to which the enthusiastic owner could belong. Whereas M.G. sports cars have always had a worldwide following, the company's saloons have often been sadly overlooked, neglected or to some people not even regarded as worthy of the M.G. name. However, there is one club solely devoted to the appreciation of the Y-type M.G., which is:

> The M.G. 'Y' Type Register
> 12 Nithsdale Road
> Liverpool
> L15 5AX

The Register was founded on January 1, 1978 at a time when Y-types were scarcely considered as worthy of preservation or restoration. Since that date a regular (now bi-monthly) newsletter has been published and is distributed worldwide. Research has uncovered much previously unknown technical and historical information about these cars (this is available to members through the 'Reference Library' scheme) and today the Register holds details of over 1,000 Y-types known still to exist. In addition, the Register has the services of a very experienced Spares Secretary who can also, if necessary, carry out work to a very high standard on members' cars.

There are three other UK-based M.G. clubs, all of which cater, in a more general way, for a cross-section of M.G. products between the late twenties and the present day. Foremost amongst these is:

> The M.G. Owners' Club
> 2/4 Station Road
> Swavesey
> Cambridge
> CB4 5QZ

The M.G. Owners' Club offers its members a very comprehensive package of membership benefits including a sophisticated glossy monthly magazine, insurance and spares discount schemes, area meetings and well-organized local and national events of all kinds. The MGOC also maintains a refreshingly broad-minded attitude towards the various types of M.G. motor car.

The original M.G. club (founded in 1930 and until the late sixties sponsored by the factory) is:

The M.G. Car Club
P.O. Box 251
Studley
Warwickshire
B80 7AT

The MGCC provides all the facilities one would expect of a large long-established club with a worldwide membership.

Finally, in the UK, there is:

The Octagon Car Club
36 Queensville Avenue
Stafford
ST17 4LS

Smaller than both the MGOC and the MGCC, the Octagon Car Club caters only for pre-1956 M.G.s, which, of course, is good news for Y-type owners! The 'Octagon' is often a very good source for the acquisition of spares.

In the United States, where, of course, M.G. cars have had a great following since the end of the Second World War, the club to contact is:

The New England M.G. 'T' Register
Drawer 220
Oneonta
New York 13820
USA

The NEMGTR, as its name suggests, concerns itself in the main with T-type and related M.G.s (such as the Y). Large concours and competitive rallies (called Gatherings of the Faithful, or GOFs) are held throughout the USA and enthusiasm is very great indeed.

Specialists

One glance at any of the glossy monthly car magazines will reveal countless numbers of 'M.G. specialists' attempting to satisfy the apparently never-ending appetite for spares amongst M.G. owners. Many of these organizations supply spares for T-type M.G.s and, as we have seen, many of the mechanical components utilized by the T-type sports cars are also to be found on the Y-type saloons and tourers. The attractiveness of the T-type sports cars and the high prices they fetch has ensured that many mechanical parts for Y-types are comparatively easy to obtain. Unfortunately, however, that same attractiveness has also ensured that those parts can be very expensive for the humble Y-type owner to purchase! The following short list of suppliers highlights organizations which have a reasonably sound knowledge of the needs of the Y-type owner when it comes to obtaining parts and are best able to supply those parts particular to the type:

A. Brier
6a Far End Lane
Honley
Huddersfield

West Yorkshire
HD7 2NS
tel: 0484 664669

N.T.G. Services
Clarence House
St. Margarets Green
Ipswich
IP4 2BN
tel: 0473 211240

and in the USA:

Moss Motors Ltd
PO Box MG
7200 Hollister Avenue
Goleta
California 93116
tel: 800-235-6954

Books

This book is the first volume to be devoted solely to the Y-type M.G. However, the model is discussed briefly in the overall context of M.G. history in the following books:

M.G. by McComb by Wilson McComb (Osprey Publishing)
The T-Series M.G.s by Graham Robson (Motor Racing Publications)
M.G. The Art of Abingdon by John Mclellan (Motor Racing Publications)
The Immortal T Series by Chris Harvey (The Oxford Illustrated Press/Haynes)

A very useful book for anyone contemplating an engine rebuild is:

Tuning & Maintenance of M.G. Cars by Philip H. Smith (G.T. Foulis/Haynes)

```
            M a g a z i n e   B i b l i o g r a p h y


  'Autocar'  Articles:

      26/10/45    The New Luvax-Girling Hydraulic Damper
      09/05/47    Meet A New M.G.
      09/05/47    Road Test No.1332
      27/06/47    Photo of car which was driven to Italy to report on the
                                        Mille Miglia ('DRX557')
      09/01/48    Making The Grades        by Michael Brown
      14/05/48    Specialised M.G. for the U.S.
      08/10/48    An Open 1¼
      04/03/49    'The Autocar' New Car Buyers' Guide
      04/03/49    Page showing 'Cars For Sale' advertisements (several 'Y's,
                      including details of a special-bodied saloon)
      11/03/49    Letter No.61802 Cars For Export (& photo of Canadian 'Y')
```

```
01/07/49    Exile In Lakeland        by John Urbane Bull
19/08/49    Day Out - and Straight Back  by Michael Brown
25/11/49    Photo of film star,Gene Tierney taking delivery of 'UMG20'
10/03/50    Photo of YT at the Chicago Sports & Outdoors Show
26/05/50    Downland Traverse        by Michael Brown
02/06/50    Photo of 'LPG796' showing how to rectify a skid
23/06/50    Border By-Pass           by Michael Brown
30/06/50    Pleasant Places In Wales by John Urbane Bull
21/07/50    East Coast Tonic         by Michael Brown
04/08/50    Green Mantled            by Michael Brown
29/09/50    Dovedale Revisited       by Michael Brown
05/01/51    Two Jumps Ahead          by Michael Brown
16/02/51    Photo of special bodied YA converted by University Motors
                                     for an American customer
06/04/51    The Rest of the 1,000
20/04/51    A Buried Treasure        by Michael Brown
15/06/51    1951 R.A.C. Rally Report.
03/08/51    Road Test No.1438
17/08/51    France on a Shoestring   by Michael Brown
31/08/51    Weekend and a Quarter!   by Michael Brown
14/09/51    Overseas Encounter       by L.A.Ayton
11/04/52    Road Test No.1461
16/05/52    Success At Silverstone (advert celebrating the first of
            three wins by 'UHK111' in the Production Touring Car Races)
23/05/52    Photo showing 'YJ3678' negotiating a hairpin in competition
20/03/53    Photo of three YBs entered for the 1953 R.A.C. Rally
08/05/53    Photo showing Swiss YB and 'YRC'
18/09/53    Photo showing 'FAG260' at Bo'ness
02/10/53    Carreg Cennen Convoy     by Michael Brown
05/03/54    Lullaby Ireland          by 'Longships'
30/04/54    Photo showing 'OZ5708' in the Circuit of Ireland Rally
23/12/55    Norwegian Venture        by 'Longships'
Various     Various letters from readers about 'Y' Types
```

'Motor' Articles:

```
28/05/47    The M.G. 1¼-Litre Saloon
28/05/47    Continental Road Test No.1c
19/05/48    Advertisement 'Maintaining the Breed'
13/10/48    A New M.G. Sports Tourer (Road Test of YT)
12/09/51    Road Test No.11/51
12/09/51    The M.G. 1¼ Litre Saloon
07/05/52    Going West Quietly
14/05/52    1952 Silverstone Meeting Report
15/10/52    The 1¼ Litre YB Saloon
23/09/53    Photo of Sir Gordon Richards taking delivery of 'YMG231'
02/12/53    'Why an American Buys a British Car' (with reference to
                                     the 'Y' Type)
```

'Motoring' Articles:

Advertisement "Dual Personality"
Advertisement "In Leicestershire or Leicester Square"

Advertisement from the cover of the July 1953 magazine.
"Well - you were right" (story about the 'Y' that was driven at over
                                               100 mph by Goldie Gardner)
"The M.G. 'YB' Saloon" (launch of new model)
"The M.G. Series 'Y' Front Suspension" by Vincent Wilson
"The Door Fittings of your Series 'M' Morris Ten" by S.F.Drake
"Understand Those Wires" by W.Topping
"The Wolseley 4/44 Rear Axle" by Brian Ash
"Windscreen Wipers" by Charles Verrall
"Supercharging M.G. XPAG Power Units - The Marshall-NORDEC installation" by
                                               W.E.Blower
"Supercharging M.G. XPAG Power Units - The Shorrock installation" by
                                               W.E.Blower
"Supercharging M.G. XPAG Power Units - The Wade installation" by
                                               W.E.Blower
"Supercharging M.G. XPAG Power Units - The Arnott installation" by
                                               W.E.Blower
"The Smiths Interior Heater" by W.E.Blower
"The Jackall Hydraulic System" by W.E.Blower
"Re-roofing your Morris 10" by H.J.Harvey A.R.Ae.S.
"Peak of Perfection" by John Penn
"The 'Trico' Windscreen Washer" by Arnold Carr
"Steps To Increased Power!" by Dennis Francis

Miscellaneous Articles:

Motor Trader   02/06/48   "M.G. 1¼ Litre Series 'Y'"
Automobile Engineer 01/49   "The 1¼ Litre M.G. Chassis"
News Exchange   08/49   photo of YT at British Car Show,Montreal
Trader Handbook   /52   three pages showing specifications
Motor Industry   08/52   M.G. 1¼ Litre Saloon (Road Test)
Motorsport   04/53   "On The Road with the 1¼ Litre M.G. Saloon"
Motorsport   09/53   "40,000 Miles with a 1¼ Litre M.G. Saloon
                                  - and how a supercharger was added"
Practical Motorist & Motorcyclist 10/58 "Decoking The 1¼ Litre Series Y"
Modern Motor   03/59   "Know Your Series 'Y'"
Restored Cars 09 & 10/76   "Drive Test - M.G. YT" by Ron Gay
Thoroughbred & Classic Cars 04/78 "M.G. YA-B" by Jonathan Wood
Practical Motorist 06/79   "Cars Worth Keeping - M.G. YB' Part 1
                                               by Phil Reckless
The Sunday Times 23/12/79   "Perelman's Last Piece"
Popular Motoring   03/81   "Love At First Sight"
Practical Motorist 09/81   "Cars Worth Keeping - M.G. YB' Part 2
                                               by Phil Reckless
M.G. Magazine Issue 11 82/83   "M.G. Saloons...with particular reference to
                                      the 'Y' Type' by Richard.L.Knudson
M.G. Magazine Issue 11 82/83   "The Year of the 'Y'" by John Dugdale
The Sacred Octagon 02/83   "The Shorrock Supercharger - Fitting & Servicing
                                               Instructions'
Practical Motorist 03/87   "Cars Worth Keeping - Morris 8 Series E"
The Sacred Octagon 10/87   "Souping the M.G." by John Christy

CHAPTER 10

Specifications

M.G. 1¼-Litre Saloon (Series Y)

Built	Abingdon-on-Thames, England, 1947-51. Total number built, 6,158.
Engine	Cast-iron block and head, aluminium sump. 4 cylinders set in line, overhead valves. Capacity, 1,250cc. Bore and stroke, 66.5mm x 90mm. Compression ratio, 7.2/7.4:1. Maximum power, 46bhp at 4,800rpm. Maximum torque, 702lb/in at 2,400rpm. Carburettor, single S.U. type H2, 1¼in. Fuel pump, S.U. type L (electric). Air cleaner, oil-wetted woven mesh type.
Transmission	Rear-wheel drive from front-mounted engine. 4-speed gearbox bolted to rear engine plate. Synchromesh on 2nd, 3rd and top gears. Clutch, Borg & Beck 7¼in dry plate. Gear ratios: Reverse 3.50:1, 1st 3.50:1, 2nd 2.07:1, 3rd 1.385:1, top 1.00:1. Final drive, three-quarter floating spiral-bevel axle 7/36. Final-drive ratio 5.143:1. Overall ratios: Reverse 18.00:1, 1st 18.00:1, 2nd 10.646:1, 3rd 7.121:1, top 5.143:1.
Suspension	Front, independent with coil springs. Rear, half-elliptic leaf springs.
Steering	Rack-and-pinion, 2.625 turns lock-to-lock. Turning circle, 35ft.
Brakes	Lockheed hydraulic, 9in diameter drums. One leading and one trailing shoe, front and rear.
Wheels and tyres	16in pressed-steel disc, 5-bolt fixings. Tyres, 5.00/5.25 x 16.
Bodywork	Designed by Gerald Palmer, pressed-steel, manufactured at Nuffield Metal Products, Birmingham. 4-door, 6-light saloon.

Dimensions and weight	Overall width, 4ft 10¼in. Overall length, 13ft 5in. Overall height, 4ft 9in. Wheelbase, 8ft 3in. Track, 3ft 11⅜in front, 4ft 2in rear. Ground clearance, 6in. Weight, 19cwt 2qr.
Electrical system	Positive earth, 12-volt, 50amp/hr battery contained in metal box in engine bay. Lucas dynamo types C39 PV, PV-2 or C45Y-V3 with Lucas RF91 or RF95 combined voltage control and fuse box and coil ignition. Headlamps, Lucas double-dip 36/36Watt. Semaphore trafficators 3W.
Performance	Maximum speed 71.4mph. Maximum speed in gears: 1st 24mph, 2nd 40mph, 3rd 60.5mph. Acceleration: 0-30mph 6.9sec, 0-50mph 16.9sec, 0-60mph 28.2sec, standing ¼-mile 23.2sec. Fuel consumption 29-36.5mpg.

M.G. 1¼-Litre Tourer (Series YT)

Built	Abingdon-on-Thames, England, 1948-50. Total number built, 877.
Engine	Cast-iron block and head, aluminium sump. 4 cylinders set in line, overhead valves. Capacity, 1,250cc. Bore and stroke, 66.5mm x 90mm. Compression ratio, 7.2/7.4:1. Maximum power, 54.4bhp at 5,200rpm. Maximum torque, 765lb/in at 2,600rpm. Carburettor, twin S.U. type H2, 1¼in. Fuel pump, S.U. type L (electric). Air cleaner, oil-bath type.
Transmission	Rear-wheel drive from front-mounted engine. 4-speed gearbox bolted to rear engine plate. Synchromesh on 2nd, 3rd and top gears. Clutch, Borg & Beck 7¼in dry plate. Gear ratios: Reverse 3.50:1, 1st 3.50:1, 2nd 2.07:1, 3rd 1.385:1, top 1.00:1. Final drive, three-quarter floating spiral-bevel axle 7/36. Final-drive ratio 5.143:1. Overall ratios: Reverse 18.00:1, 1st 18.00:1, 2nd 10.646:1, 3rd 7.121:1, top 5.143:1.
Suspension	Front, independent with coil springs. Rear, half-elliptic leaf springs.
Steering	Rack-and-pinion, 2.625 turns lock-to-lock. Turning circle, 35ft.
Brakes	Lockheed hydraulic, 9in diameter drums. One leading and one trailing shoe, front and rear.
Wheels and tyres	16in pressed-steel disc, 5-bolt fixings. Tyres, 5.00/5.25 x 16.
Bodywork	Designed by Gerald Palmer, pressed steel with coachbuilt doors, manufactured partly at Nuffield Metal Products, Birmingham and partly at Abingdon. 2-door convertible with soft top.

Dimensions and weight	Overall width, 4ft 11in. Overall length, 13ft 8in. Overall height, 4ft 10½in. Wheelbase, 8ft 3in. Track, 3ft 11⅜in front, 4ft 2in rear. Ground clearance, 6in. Weight, 18cwt 3qr.
Electrical system	Positive earth, 12-volt, 50amp/hr battery contained in metal box in engine bay. Lucas dynamo type C45Y-V3 with Lucas RF95 combined voltage control and fuse box and coil ignition. Headlamps, Lucas double-dip 36/36Watt. Flashing direction indicators on cetain cars for the US.
Performance	Maximum speed 76mph. Maximum speed in gears: 1st 25mph, 2nd 40mph, 3rd 58mph. Acceleration: 0-30mph 6.7sec, 0-50mph 16.2sec, 0-60mph 25.2 sec, standing ¼-mile 23.1sec. Fuel consumption 32mpg.

M.G. 1¼-Litre Saloon (Series YB)

Built	Abingdon-on-Thames, England, 1952-53. Total number built, 1,301.
Engine	Cast-iron block and head, aluminium sump. 4 cylinders set in line, overhead valves. Capacity, 1,250cc. Bore and stroke, 66.5mm x 90mm. Compression ratio, 7.2/7.4:1. Maximum power, 46bhp at 4,800rpm. Maximum torque, 702lb/in at 2,400rpm. Carburettor, single S.U. type H2, 1¼in. Fuel pump, S.U. type L (electric). Air cleaner, oil-wetted woven mesh type.
Transmission	Rear-wheel drive from front-mounted engine. 4-speed gearbox bolted to rear engine plate. Synchromesh on 2nd, 3rd and top gears. Clutch, Borg & Beck 8in dry plate*. Gear ratios: Reverse 3.50:1, 1st 3.50:1, 2nd 2.07:1, 3rd 1.385:1, top 1.00:1. Final drive, semi-floating hypoid rear axle 8/41. Final-drive ratio 5.125:1. Overall ratios: Reverse 17.937:1, 1st 17.937:1, 2nd 10.608:1, 3rd 7.098:1, top 5.125:1.
Suspension	Front, independent with coil springs. Rear, half-elliptic leaf springs.
Steering	Rack-and-pinion, 2.625 turns lock-to-lock. Turning circle, 33ft 6in.
Brakes	Lockheed hydraulic, 9in diameter drums. Twin leading shoes front, one leading and one trailing shoe rear.
Wheels and tyres	15in pressed-steel disc, 5-bolt fixings. Tyres, 5.50 x 15.
Bodywork	Designed by Gerald Palmer, pressed steel, manufactured at Nuffield Metal Products, Birmingham. 4-door 6-light saloon.
Dimensions and weight	Overall width, 4ft 11in. Overall length, 13ft 8in. Overall

	height, 4ft 9in. Wheelbase, 8ft 3in. Track, 3ft 11³⁄₈in front, 4ft 2in rear. Ground clearance, 6in. Weight, 20cwt 3qr.
Electrical system	Positive earth, 12-volt, 51amp/hr battery contained in metal box in engine bay. Lucas dynamo type C39 PV-2 with Lucas RB106 voltage control unit and coil ignition. Headlamps, Lucas double-dip 42/36Watt. Semaphore trafficators 3W.
Performance	Maximum speed 71.4mph. Maximum speed in gears: 1st 22mph, 2nd 40mph, 3rd 59mph. Acceleration: 0-30mph 6.9sec, 0-50mph 18.4sec, 0-60mph 30.4 sec, standing ¹⁄₄-mile 24.5sec. Fuel consumption 26.5mpg.

*8in clutch introduced in 1951 on last batch of YAs with first XPAG/SC2 engines.

APPENDIX 1

Existing cars – important statistics

YAs	544	Scotland	24
YBs	245	Republic of South Africa	23
YTs	171	Wales	21
YRCs	3	New Zealand	17
Specials/Composites	11	Eire	10
Unknown (mainly saloons)	73	Canada	9
		Singapore	9
Total number of existing cars	1,047	Malaysia	8
Positively identified	825	Switzerland	7
Others (tentatively identified)	222	Hong Kong	4
		Northern Ireland	4
		Madeira	3
Cars identified by chassis number:		Channel Islands	3
1947	39	Cyprus	2
1948	60	Belgium	2
1949	171	Federal Republic of Germany	2
1950	136	Zimbabwe	2
1951	53	Malta	2
1952	54	Japan	2
1953	76	Liechtenstein	1
		Denmark	1
Total	589	Bangladesh	1
		Portugal	1
Number of current owners	681	Isle of Man	1
		France	1
Number of cars in each country:		Sri Lanka	1
England	524	Luxembourg	1
Australia	211	Norway	1
U.S.A.	124	*(32 countries)*	
Netherlands	25		

APPENDIX 2

List of all existing cars

1947		
Y 0263	Cheshire	England
Y 0264	London	England
Y 0296	Virginia	USA
Y 0340	Staffordshire	England
Y 0343	Cambridgeshire	England
Y 0358	Kent	England
Y 0361	Derbyshire	England
Y 0364	Buckinghamshire	England
Y 0436	Connecticut	USA
Y 0481	Oxfordshire	England
Y 0485	Sussex	England
Y 0512	Cornwall	England
Y 0559	NSW	Australia
Y 0596	Queensland	Australia
Y 0602	Avon	England
Y 0606	Schwarzenburg	Switzerland
Y 0614	Nottinghamshire	England
Y 0672	Cornwall	England
Y 0673	Lancashire	England
Y 0674	Clwyd	Wales
Y 0734	Avon	England
Y 0785	Oxfordshire	England
Y 0795	Washington DC	USA
Y 0811	London	England
Y 0833	New York	USA
Y 0865	NSW	Australia
Y 0883	Dunedin	NZ
Y 0890	NSW	Australia
Y 0972	Queensland	Australia
Y 1000	NSW	Australia
Y 1041	–	Singapore
Y 1052	Yorkshire	England
Y 1057	NSW	Australia
Y 1064	NSW	Australia
Y 1091	Victoria	Australia
Y 1098	Victoria	Australia
Y 1126	Victoria	Australia
Y 1138	ACT	Australia
Y 1141	Tasmania	Australia
1948		
Y 1168	Victoria	Australia
Y 1174	Victoria	Australia
Y 1175	Victoria	Australia
Y 1184	Victoria	Australia
Y 1209	Essex	England
Y 1221	Victoria	Australia
Y 1279	Victoria	Australia
Y 1280	?	Australia
Y 1292	Victoria	Australia
Y 1327	Co.Down	NI
Y 1336	Ontario	Canada

Y 1366RC	Obere Platten	Lic'stein
Y 1367RC	?	Switzerland
Y 1380RC	?	Switzerland
Y 1429	Dunedin	NZ
Y 1441	Dunedin	NZ
Y 1442	Christchurch	NZ
Y 1443	Victoria	Australia
Y 1468	Funchal	Madeira
Y 1469	?	England
Y 1488	Victoria	Australia
Y 1505	Devon	England
Y 1507	?	England
Y 1535	Victoria	Australia
Y 1552	Victoria	Australia
Y 1568	Victoria	Australia
Y 1586	?	England
Y 1592	NSW	Australia
Y 1633	Weltevreden Pk	RSA
Y 1634	Somerset	England
Y 1637	Oberegg	Switzerland
Y 1641	Victoria	Australia
Y 1662	Sussex	England
Y 1674	Durban	RSA
Y 1713	Dunedin	NZ
Y 1753	Victoria	Australia
Y 1775	Avon	England
Y 1782	Victoria	Austrália
Y 1800	Victoria	Australia
Y 1804	California	USA
Y 1805	California	USA
Y 1812	Surrey	England
Y 1855	Victoria	Australia
Y 1924T	?	Neth
Y 1929	Dorset	England
Y 1932	Victoria	Australia
Y 1935	NSW	Australia
Y 1948	Victoria	Australia
Y 1951	–	Hong Kong
Y 1966	Florida	USA
Y 1978	Victoria	Australia
Y 2005	Victoria	Australia
Y 2031T	New York	USA
Y 2056	Lyndhurst	RSA
Y 2074	Durban	RSA
Y 2122	Glamorgan	Wales
Y 2137T	–	Singapore
Y 2172T	Durban	RSA
Y 2193	WA	Australia
Y 2194	Delft	Neth
1949		
Y 2300	NSW	Australia
Y 2313	Somerset	England
Y 2314	Surrey	England
Y 2332	S.A.	Australia

Y 2367	Virginia	USA	Y 3208T	Victoria	Australia
Y 2375	?	USA ?	Y 3218	Victoria	Australia
Y 2401	Victoria	Australia	Y 3230	Victoria	Australia
Y 2412	NSW	Australia	Y 3285T	Quebec	Canada
Y 2425T	Bloemfontein	RSA	Y 3286T	Essex	England
Y 2431T	?	?	Y 3287T	N.Carolina	USA
Y 2459	Worcestershire	England	Y 3290T	Somerset West	RSA
Y 2467T	Bulawayo	Zimbabwe	Y 3299T	NSW	Australia
Y 2472T	?	RSA	Y 3300T	Victoria	Australia
Y 2492	Hastings	NZ	Y 3301T	NSW	Australia
Y 2506T	?	USA	Y 3335T	?	England ?
Y 2509T	Massachusetts	USA	Y 3336T	Glos.	England
Y 2529	Durban	RSA	Y 3343T	New York	USA
Y 2532	Hampshire	England	Y 3360	NSW	Australia
Y 2582T	Durban	RSA	Y 3363	California	USA
Y 2587T	Boksburg	RSA	Y 3374T	Derbyshire	England
Y 2596T	S.A.	Australia	Y 3377T	?	USA
Y 2598	Merseyside	England	Y 3387T	Victoria	Australia
Y 2617T	Hertfordshire	England	Y 3391T	?	Singapore
Y 2618T	Berkshire	England	Y 3392	Queensland	Australia
Y 2620T	NSW	Australia	Y 3393	?	USA
Y 2645	Alva	Scotland	Y 3410	Clwyd	Wales
Y 2664T	Dyfed	Wales	Y 3412	Yorkshire	England
Y 2675	California	USA	Y 3414	Victoria	Australia
Y 2677	Connecticut	USA	Y 3425T	Norfolk	England
Y 2685	Victoria	Australia	Y 3428	Tasmania	Australia
Y 2687	NSW	Australia	Y 3430T	?	RSA
Y 2703T	?	Australia	Y 3441T	?	?
Y 2710	Essex	England	Y 3443	Hampshire	England
Y 2716	–	Singapore	Y 3444	Cornwall	England
Y 2735T	Massachusetts	USA	Y 3449	Victoria	Australia
Y 2739T	Ontario	Canada	Y 3452	W.A.	Australia
Y 2740T	Michigan	USA	Y 3453	Victoria	Australia
Y 2745T	Cork	Eire	Y 3458	NSW	Australia
Y 2788	ACT	Australia	Y 3459	Derbyshire	England
Y 2795	Victoria	Australia	Y 3462	Co.Dublin	Eire
Y 2814T	California	USA	Y 3463	Victoria	Australia
Y 2834	Victoria	Australia	Y 3465T	Alberta	Canada
Y 2851T	Oregon	USA	Y 3470T	?	England
Y 2853T	New York ?	USA	Y 3480T	Queensland	Australia
Y 2868	S.A.	Australia	Y 3498	Victoria	Australia
Y 2883T	NSW	Australia	Y 3523T	Kent	England
Y 2893	NSW	Australia	Y 3524T	S.A.	Australia
Y 2906	Victoria	Australia	Y 3534	ACT	Australia
Y 2953	NSW	Australia	Y 3540	Cumbria	England
Y 2967	Durban	RSA	Y 3552	Victoria	Australia
Y 3030T	Massachusetts	USA	Y 3569T	?	England ?
Y 3061T	?	RSA	Y 3578	NSW	Australia
Y 3073T	Florida	USA	Y 3581T	NSW	Australia
Y 3074T	New York	USA	Y 3582	NSW	Australia
Y 3075T	Oregon	USA	Y 3601	NSW	Australia
Y 3102	Co.Dublin	Eire	Y 3623T	Queensland	Australia
Y 3105T	Ontario	Canada	Y 3626T	Worcestershire	England
Y 3106T	Ontario	Canada	Y 3629	Victoria	Australia
Y 3117	Queensland	Australia	Y 3667T	Victoria	Australia
Y 3120	W.A.	Australia	Y 3681	Lancashire	England
Y 3143T	?	USA	Y 3698	NSW	Australia
Y 3144T	Massachusetts	USA	Y 3700T	Queensland	Australia
Y 3173T	?	USA	Y 3706T	Queensland	Australia
Y 3177T	Ontario	Canada	Y 3737T	Victoria	Australia
Y 3187	Victoria	Australia	Y 3738T	S.A.	Australia
Y 3192	NSW	Australia	Y 3741T	Victoria	Australia
Y 3200	Hampshire	England	Y 3752	Victoria	Australia
Y 3205	Victoria	Australia	Y 3776	Suffolk	England

Y 3779T	NSW	Australia	Y 4418	Kent	England
Y 3790	NSW	Australia	Y 4439	Victoria	Australia
Y 3808	Leicestershire	England	Y 4452T	W. Midlands	England
Y 3810	Victoria	Australia	Y 4457T	?	USA
Y 3819T	?	England	Y 4458T	Florida	USA
Y 3823T	Victoria	Australia	Y 4465	Ohio	USA
Y 3841	Victoria	Australia	Y 4470	NSW	Australia
Y 3846	Victoria	Australia	Y 4471	NSW	Australia
Y 3861	NSW	Australia	Y 4506	Victoria	Australia
Y 3915T	NSW	Australia	Y 4507	Durban	RSA
Y 3930	NSW	Australia	Y 4511	Victoria	Australia
Y 3947	Aberdeen	Scotland	Y 4517	Victoria	Australia
Y 3965T	Oberwil	Switzerland	Y 4529	Essex	England
Y 3966	NSW	Australia	Y 4535T	Florida	USA
Y 3974T	NSW	Australia	Y 4558	Victoria	Australia
Y 3975T	NSW	Australia	Y 4570?	Surrey	England
Y 3981	Cheshire	England	Y 4593	Surrey	England
Y 4037	NSW	Australia	Y 4621T	Queensland	Australia
Y 4040	NSW	Australia	Y 4626	?	England
Y 4054	Victoria	Australia	Y 4629	California	USA
Y 4067T	NSW	Australia	Y 4634	Durban	RSA
Y 4100T	?	?	Y 4664T	NSW	Australia
Y 4119T	Victoria	Australia	Y 4681	NSW	Australia
Y 4120T	Victoria	Australia	Y 4699	Victoria	Australia
Y 4142	Merseyside	England	Y 4725T	?	USA
Y 4144	New Jersey	USA	Y 4738	Victoria	Australia
Y 4146	Victoria	Australia	Y 4739	Victoria	Australia
Y 4161T	California	USA	Y 4754	–	Singapore
Y 4162T	Den Haag	Neth	Y 4788	Tasmania	Australia
Y 4167T	NSW	Australia	Y 4792	Cardiff	Wales
Y 4175T	?	?	Y 4827T	Merseyside	England
Y 4176T	Rhode Island	USA	Y 4831T	Ohio	USA
Y 4188	Queensland	Australia	Y 4832T	Georgia	USA
Y 4189	Queensland	Australia	Y 4833T	Missouri	USA
Y 4216	NSW	Australia	Y 4837	NSW	Australia
Y 4217T	?	USA	Y 4844	Oxfordshire	England
Y 4219T	Iowa	USA	Y 4880	California	USA
Y 4220T	Birrwil	Switzerland	Y 4884	Victoria	Australia
Y 4223T	Victoria	Australia	Y 4888	Sussex	England
			Y 4941	Norfolk	England
			Y 4945	Gloucestershire	England
1950			Y 4953	Hampshire	England
			Y 4962T	?	USA
Y 4249	Gloucestershire	England	Y 4965T	Massachusetts	USA
Y 4252	Norfolk	England	Y 4984	Victoria	Australia
Y 4260T	Victoria	Australia	Y 4988	Gloucestershire	England
Y 4264T	Dumfries	Scotland	Y 5011	Pennsylvania	USA
Y 4273	NSW	Australia	Y 5015	?	Malaysia
Y 4276	Kent	England	Y 5020	Louisiana	USA
Y 4297	Victoria	Australia	Y 5039T	Victoria	Australia
Y 4298	Victoria	Australia	Y 5063	Sussex	England
Y 4302	Victoria	Australia	Y 5100	Lancashire	England
Y 4318T	NSW	Australia	Y 5129T	W. A.	Australia
Y 4320T	NSW	Australia	Y 5139T	NSW	Australia
Y 4321T	?	?	Y 5142T	Tasmania	Australia
Y 4327T	Christchurch	NZ	Y 5150T	Tasmania	Australia
Y 4330	Cambridgeshire	England	Y 5156T	Victoria	Australia
Y 4361	Sussex	England	Y 5162	Middlesex	England
Y 4368T	New York	USA	Y 5174	Michigan	USA
Y 4372T	New York	USA	Y 5199	Gloucestershire	England
Y 4384T	?	?	Y 5205	Surrey	England
Y 4389	NSW	Australia	Y 5209	Victoria	Australia
Y 4391	Hampshire	England	Y 5222	Bedfordshire	England
Y 4407	Hampshire	England	Y 5232	Cumbria	England

Y 5246	Devon	England	Y 6459	Cambridgeshire	England
Y 5288	Tyne & Wear	England	Y 6479	Bloemfontein	RSA
Y 5294	Bedfordshire	England	Y 6488	Derbyshire	England
Y 5312	Avon	England	Y 6503	W.Midlands	England
Y 5330	Hertfordshire	England	Y 6506	NSW	Australia
Y 5340	Victoria	Australia	Y 6522	?	Neth ?
Y 5343	S.A.	Australia	Y 6531	Victoria	Australia
Y 5349	Lancashire	England	Y 6545	Tyne & Wear	England
Y 5393	Berkshire	England	Y 6557	Middlesex	England
Y 5403	Hampshire	England	Y 6566	Surrey	England
Y 5445	Kent	England	Y 6610	Hertfordshire	England
Y 5460	California	USA	Y 6615	N.Humberside	England
Y 5476	Avon	England	Y 6628	Essex	England
Y 5508	NSW	Australia	Y 6686	Yorkshire	England
Y 5528	California	USA	Y 6698	Victoria	Australia
Y 5537	Kent	England	Y 6726	Warwickshire	England
Y 5539	Victoria	Australia	Y 6769	Stirling	Scotland
Y 5612	Gtr.Manchester	England	Y 6774	NSW	Australia
Y 5633	Essex	England	Y 6783	Leicestershire	England
Y 5660	Merseyside	England	Y 6785	Oxfordshire	England
Y 5692	Staffordshire	England	Y 6791	Gloucestershire	England
Y 5725	Virginia	USA	Y 6814	London	England
Y 5729	Cheshire	England	Y 6882	Derbyshire	England
Y 5765	Kent	England	Y 6906	Co.Durham	England
Y 5775	Yorkshire	England	Y 6914	California	USA
Y 5776	California	USA	Y 6918	Leicestershire	England
Y 5796	Middlesex	England	Y 6969	Yorkshire	England
Y 5802	Hampshire	England	Y 7004	Avon	England
Y 5831	Tyne & Wear	England	Y 7011	Sussex	England
Y 5910	Gtr.Manchester	England	Y 7012	Sussex	England
Y 5911	Sussex	England	Y 7015	Hampshire	England
Y 5915	Derbyshire	England	Y 7028	Sussex	England
Y 5921	Hampshire	England	Y 7051	Surrey	England
Y 5927	NSW	Australia	Y 7056	Cumbria	England
Y 5968	Essex	England	Y 7063	Avon	England
Y 5978	Harlingen	Neth	Y 7066	Cheshire	England
Y 6003	Gloucestershire	England	Y 7116	Norfolk	England
Y 6012	London	England	Y 7117	Lancashire	England
Y 6041	Middlesex	England	Y 7122	Sussex	England
Y 6074	W.A.	Australia	Y 7166	?	England
Y 6085	Victoria	Australia	Y 7193	Cambridgeshire	England
Y 6105	Victoria	Australia	Y 7207	Lincolnshire	England
Y 6126	Tasmania	Australia	Y 7225	Avon	England
Y 6146	Sussex	England			
Y 6197	NSW	Australia			
Y 6201	W.A.	Australia			
Y 6213	Yorkshire	England	**1952**		
Y 6215	Victoria	Australia			
Y 6227	Sussex	England	YB0251	?	England?
Y 6244	Virginia	USA	YB0264	Sussex	England
Y 6271	Herefordshire	England	YB0267	Worcestershire	England
			YB0303	Stranraer	Scotland
1951			YB0305	Kent	England
			YB0308	Kent	England
Y 6315	?	England	YB0318	Florida	USA
Y 6325	Surrey	England	YB0328	Surrey	England
Y 6326	Victoria	Australia	YB0337	Virginia	USA
Y 6332	Clwyd	Wales	YB0350	Tyne & Wear	England
Y 6381	Victoria	Australia	YB0354	Sussex	England
Y 6389	Merseyside	England	YB0362	Essex	England
Y 6407	California	USA	YB0365	Bucks	England
Y 6412	Victoria	Australia	YB0382	Yorkshire	England
Y 6420	Hampshire	England	YB0393	Dorset	England
Y 6421	Fife	Scotland	YB0398	Ayr	Scotland

YB0402	Fife	Scotland		YB1063	Avon	England
YB0414	Kent	England		YB1084	Sussex	England
YB0446	?	England		YB1094	Lancashire	England
YB0456	S.Glamorgan	Wales		YB1099	New York	USA
YB0475	Middlesex	England		YB1100	Shropshire	England
YB0481	Warwickshire	England		YB1117	Oxfordshire	England
YB0485	Yorkshire	England		YB1141	Dyfed	Wales
YB0511	Nebraska	USA		YB1148	Worcestershire	England
YB0512	Cheshire	England		YB1154	New Jersey	USA
YB0534	Surrey	England		YB1169	Staffordshire	England
YB0545	Warwickshire	England		YB1170	Lancashire	England
YB0551	?	?		YB1177	Northamptonshire	England
YB0552	Yorkshire	England		YB1178	E.Lothian	Scotland
YB0556	Somerset	England		YB1179	Berkshire	England
YB0566	Lincolnshire	England		YB1184	Co.Durham	England
YB0567	Jersey	CI		YB1189	?	England
YB0593	Kent	England		YB1204	Essex	England
YB0601	Shropshire	England		YB1206	California	USA
YB0610	Yorkshire	England		YB1216	Staffordshire	England
YB0620	W.Midlands	England		YB1240	Oxfordshire	England
YB0631	Wiltshire	England		YB1241	NSW	Australia
YB0647	Merseyside	England		YB1245	Nottinghamshire	England
YB0651	Merseyside	England		YB1248	Leicestershire	England
YB0660	Cleveland	England		YB1262	Middlesex	England
YB0662	Yorkshire	England		YB1267	Sussex	England
YB0672	W.Midlands	England		YB1275	New York ?	USA
YB0686	Yorkshire	England		YB1277	Cleveland	England
YB0696	Suffolk	England		YB1296	Paisley	Scotland
YB0752	Boksburg	RSA		YB1300	London	England
YB0762	Yorkshire	England		YB1307	California	USA
YB0831	Merseyside	England		YB1320	?	England
YB0850	Washington	USA		YB1327	Avon	England
YB0874	Bucks	England		YB1340	Ontario	Canada
YB0885	Sussex	England		YB1342	Cornwall	England
YB0900	London	England		YB1362	Gwent	Wales
YB0920	Lincolnshire	England		YB1372	Surrey	England
YB0922	Oxfordshire	England		YB1379	s'Hertogenbosch	Neth
YB0923	?	England		YB1393	Yorkshire	England
				YB1401	Wurselen	FRG
				YB1405	Lancashire	England
1953				YB1411	Suffolk	England
				YB1431	Aberdeen	Scotland
YB0930	Colorado	USA		YB1465	Jersey	C.I.
YB0944	Buckinghamshire	England		YB1470	Caithness	Scotland
YB0952	Louisiana	USA		YB1477	Yorkshire	England
YB0955	Middlesex	England		YB1493	Staffordshire	England
YB0962	Nottinghamshire	England		YB1496	Cheshire	England
YB0970	W.Midlands	England		YB1506	Lancashire	England
YB0991	Yorkshire	England		YB1508	Ohio	USA
YB0999	S.Carolina	USA		YB1512	New Jersey	USA
YB1020	Kilmarnock	Scotland		YB1516	?	England?
YB1023	S.A.	Australia		YB1520	S.Carolina	USA
YB1029	Virginia	USA		YB1524	Cumbria	England
YB1041	Co. Antrim	NI		YB1533	Surrey	England
YB1042	M.Glamorgan	Wales		YB1535	Virginia	USA
YB1045	Surrey	England		YB1540	Staffordshire	England
YB1050	Northamptonshire	England		YB1544	Yorkshire	England
YB1054	Kent	England		YB1547	Staffordshire	England
YB1060	Surrey	England		YB1551	?	England

Note: In the above listings,YT chassis numbers are suffixed 'T' and the Reinbolt &
Christe tourers are suffixed 'RC',for ease of reference only; the chassis numbers
of these cars are not presented in this way on the cars' identification plates.
See appendix (iii) for further explanation.

APPENDIX 3

Points of originality & production figures

Year by year production was as follows:

Series Y:	Chassis numbers	
1947	Y 0251 to Y 1150	900 cars
1948	Y 1151 to Y 2208	1,058 cars
1949	Y 2209 to Y 4239	2,031 cars
1950	Y 4240 to Y 6284	2,045 cars
1951	Y 6285 to Y 7285	1,001 cars

The tourer version (the YT) was produced between 1948 and 1950 and chassis numbers were included in the normal Y series above. There were 6,158 Y saloons and 877 tourers built.

Series YB:	Chassis numbers	
1952	YB 0251 to YB 0929*	679 cars
1953	YB 0930* to YB 1551	622 cars

* this information is unconfirmed.

There were 1,301 YBs in all and a total of 8,336 Y-types of all variants.

The following 'CKD' cars were exported by Abingdon:

1947	16
1948	68
1949	124*
1950	76
1952	28
1953	8

* 108 YA plus 16 YT. The 1952 and 1953 cars were YBs. All the cars delivered were RHD examples. Total 424. Many of these cars went to Eire, to the Irish distributor.

A total of 11 cars (including two YBs), all RHD, were exported by Abingdon in chassis only form – 9 in 1948, one in 1952, one in 1953.

4,440 saloons were known to have been sold in the U.K. 3,019 (40.47%) were therefore exported.

Chassis numbers can be found on a plate affixed to the left-hand side of the car's battery box. This is not always an infallible source of information however and, if you wish to verify the chassis number of a car, it may also be found stamped on the outer face of the left-hand chassis member just behind the front bumper fixing stud. There is reason to believe, however, that some chassis escaped number stamping. Points to note about chassis number presentation are:

1: There is one known example of a chassis number presented thus: Y 0795X. This car was an early example exported to Cyprus.

2: YT chassis numbers are presented thus:

Y/T	RHD for home	Speedometer in MPH
Y/T/EXL	LHD for export	Speedometer in KPH
Y/T/EXR	RHD for export	Speedometer in MPH
Y/T/EXR/K	RHD for export	Speedometer in KPH
Y/T/EXL/M	LHD for export	Speedometer in MPH
Y/T/EX(U)	LHD for USA	Speedometer in MPH

3: Six left-hand-drive saloons (all YAs) are known to exist. The chassis number of one example is known to be Y 5174 EXLU.

One recorded LHD YA has engine number XPAG/SC/LHX14975.

Many BMC replacement Gold Seal engines have found their way into Y-types over the years. Examples of such engine numbers follow:

XPAG/SC/B34681   XPAG/SC/G73602
XPAG/SC2/C91900   XPAG/SC2/D06214
XPAG/TR/B50599

There appears not to be a decipherable pattern to the allocation of these engine numbers. Some Y-types have also been fitted later in their lives with XPAW engines from

Wolseley 4/44s. These engines are virtually identical to the XPAG series, the only outwardly noticeable difference being that the oil dipstick tube is on the opposite side of the engine block to that of the XPAG.

The following engines have the letters RS as part of their engine numbers:

RS 19094	fitted to YB 0696.
RS 4223	was once fitted to Y 5802.
RS 4457	fitted to Y 7028.

These markings have been positively confirmed and it is tentatively suggested that this desgnation means that the engine has been re-sleeved. Alternatively the designation may be proper to the Hepolite piston and piston ring numbering system and may refer to the type and size of pistons or rings fitted to a rebuilt engine. On the last of the three cars mentioned above, the RS 4457 is stamped on the original engine number plate on the lower right-hand side of the engine block. The car's battery box plate shows XPAG/SC/16838, the car's original engine.

The body number is to be found on a small plate fastened to the left-hand side of the scuttle. In many cases these seem to have disappeared over the years. Examples which follow will hopefully serve to illustrate the body numbering system. It will also be noticed that the saloon bodies were not necessarily allocated to chassis in strict chronological order of build. YT bodies were an exception to this and had their own, more logical, body numbering system.

Series Y:

Body number	Chassis number
158/206	Y 0358
1339/1427	Y 1637
2669/2732	Y 3498
2392/2773	Y 3534
4487/4612	Y 5692
4391/4461	Y 5765

Why there should be two number groups is not clear but the solution may be Morris-related (of which more later).

Series YB:

Body number	Chassis number
5936/150	YB 0305
6135/610	YB 0647
7124/1334	YB 1524

Here it is obvious that the first number group is a consecutive number dating from the beginning of production in 1947, whilst the second number group relates solely to the YB and dates from 1952. The first group of four numbers in the saloon body number is also to be found on a small plate at the rear of the sunroof. The sunroof has to be removed for this plate to be seen.

Series YT:

Body number	Chassis number
19604-185	Y/T/EX(U) 2509
19630-212	Y/T/EXR 2617
45022-342	Y/T/EXR 3030
45013/356	Y/T/EXL 3075
53094-766	Y/T/EXR 4372
53216-875	Y/T/EX(U) 4833

The second number group of the YT body numbers is simply a sequence starting at 1 and ending at 903 (although there were only 877 cars built, at least 903 bodies were completed, car number Y/T/EXR 4965 having the body number 53240-903). Even then the sequence does not proceed in strict order. Note that in the first number group the first two digits are 19, 45 or 53. The significance of these groups is not known. They do not relate to the three years of production of the YT.

What can best be described as the 'body code' (for its precise significance remains a mystery) can be found on a plate affixed to the engine bay bulkhead. Above this is a plate which gives the body type and this is fairly straightforward. Type B281 – Y & YB. Type B282 – YT. The body codes however are a different matter. These seem to have been very rarely recorded in full by owners the author has contacted over the years and thus the solution to their meaning has so far eluded him. To date only eighteen recorded 'body codes' have come to light from which to try and piece together a meaningful pattern. However, a theory has been put forward which goes some of the way towards explain-ing the significance of these number. In all probability Type B281 bodies (those for the saloons) were manufactured at the Nuffield Bodies plant in Birmingham. They were, after all, basically Morris 8 Series E bodyshells and there were large numbers of 8s built both before and after the Second World War. All these basic bodyshells, whether destined eventually for Morris 8s or for Y-types possibly shared a common type-numbering sequence and it is only an abstracted part of this which we see when examining the 'body codes' of Y-tyes.

Shown below are some examples of this 'body code' which will serve to illustrate the attempt which follows to partially deciper their meaning:

Chassis number	Body code		Body number
Y 0672		–	375/521
	1.25 MG	375	
	No.364	Z8693	
Y 1929		–	1617/1710
	1.25 MG	1617	
	1617	Z8693	
Y 1951	MGA 1763		1702/1732
	1.25 MG	1702	
	1702	Z8693	
Y 3776		–	2885/2950
	1.25 MG	2885	
	No.2885	Z8693	
Y 4844		–	3891/–
	–	–	
	761	SR.Z11165	
Y4888		–	3732/3705
	–	–	
	No.602	SR.Z11165	
Y4988		–	3755/–
	–	–	
	No.33	SR.Z11165	
Y5460	–	– –	
	–	–	
		SL.Z10412	
Y 5537		–	4248/4237
	1.25 MG	4248	
	No.218	SL.Z10412	
Y 6146		–	4819/4819
	1.25 MG	4819	
	No.389	SR.Z12092	
YB 0752		–	6369/575
	1.25 MG	6369	
	No.512	SR.Z12592	
YB 0955		–	6569/773
	1.25 MG	6569	
	No.712	SR.Z12592	
YB 1524	BMG 928		7124/1334
	1.25 MG	7124	
	No.278	Z12488	

The first line of the body code would appear to show that MGA = YA and BMG = YB. On the second line it is fairly obvious that 1.25 MG relates to 1¼-litre M.G. The four-figure number following this is always the same as the first group of four numbers in the body number proper.

The third line of numbers proves less easy to decipher but holds more interest. Let us take the last grouping of letters and numbers first. It might seem reasonable to the casual observer that SR.Z could indicate a right-hand-drive car whereas SL.Z might apply to a left-hand-drive car. Neat as this might be as a solution, however, this is not the case for neither Y 5460 nor Y 5537 (listed above) are LHD cars and only a very small number of LHD saloons (all YAs) are thought to have been made (one, incidentally, has the body code SR.Z11165). No, the real answer is somewhat more complex.

There is evidence to suggest that Z8693 relates to the first type of YA body; that which incorporates the battery box offset to the near-side (left) of the car. The grouping which follows on from this is SR.Z11165 which would seem to apply to the YA body after its first major modification (the movement of the battery box to a central location; the last YA to be equipped with an offset battery box was Y4459). SL.Z10412 should therefore relate to a further modification and SR.Z12092 to yet another. It is not known to what modifications these last two groupings relate.

Now we come on to the YBs. The YB body had to have a larger spare wheel compartment opening to accommodate wider tyres. Thus, it is conjectured, body sub-type SR.Z12592 was introduced. But the YB body seems to have undergone a later modification to Z12488 standard (again, it is not presently known to what modification this last alphanumeric grouping relates).

The first grouping of figures on the last line of the body code plate (often, but not always, preceded by 'No.') would seem to be a sequential numbering from the occasion of the last modification (of course, when they arrived at Abingdon bodies were not allocated to chassis in strict sequential or chronological order of build, and this explains the discrepancies and anomalies which will be apparent when the listing above is examined closely).

One statement regarding these body codes which can be made with some degree of certainty however is that they do not relate in any way to the exterior colours in which the cars were originally finished, nor to the colour of upholstery fitted.

The original shape and dimensions of the front and rear bumpers of these cars is still a controversial subject and because most cars during their lives have acquired a variety of non-original bumpers, no definitive answer has yet emerged. What differences there are exist mainly in end shape (pointed or rounded) and invariably this is often a matter of degree which is hard to judge without the presence of many different cars at one location at the same time. It is possible that differences in shape exist between front and rear YT bumpers and even between the front and rear over-riders.

Research has also shown that it is difficult to be categorical as regards originality of parts as there were many instances of 'special equipment' being specified by the customer and, additionally, these cars retained an element of personalized building although they were built on a production line and with pressed steel bodies. It has been found, for instance, that there are significant variations in the length of bonnet panels fitted to Ys. No pattern has emerged to explain this occurrence and it is thought that this is simply a result of panels being fitted to cars on an individual basis to match the distance between the radiator grille and the bulkhead. The XPAG engine was also the subject of modification throughout its life and, although the change from SC to SC2 has been covered in the appropriate chapter, it should be borne in mind that from year to year there were many small improvements made.

Lastly a word about UMG and YMG registration plates. The UMG batch of registration marks seems to have been reserved for the exclusive use of long-time London M.G. dealer, University Motors. The registrations seem to have been allocated chronologically (with one or two exceptions) to Y-types and T-types throughout the late 1940s and early 1950s. A selection of Y-type examples will suffice to show the pattern:

Reg number	Chassis number	Reg number	Chassis number
UMG 50	Y 3443	UMG 600	YB 0264
UMG 118	Y 4407	UMG 803	YB 0631
UMG 422	Y 7012		

UMG 422 and at least one other example have rather attractive small *University Motors* plaques affixed to their dashboards. It is not known whether every UMG car was originally so adorned but it does seem to be the case that University Motors had a tradition of making the cars they sold that little bit special by adding optional extras. Following the UMGs, a batch of YMG registrations was used on late YBs:

Reg number	Chassis number
YMG 5	YB 0885
YMG 124	YB 1204
YMG 186	YB 1277

An official publication in a red cover (similar to the Owners' Handbooks and Workshop Manuals) is entitled *The First 500 Miles on your new M.G. 1¼ Litre*. This is an 18-page booklet which includes a lubrication chart. It was apparently given to owners when they took delivery of their new cars. When the first 500 miles was completed the owner was apparently supposed to return the booklet to the factory and he would then be issued with an official Workshop Manual. This procedure may explain why these booklets are very rare nowadays.

On page 34 of a certain edition of the *YA Owners' Handbook* (thought to be a 1950 issue) reference is made to there being 'a spare quart of N.O.L. Engine Oil' supplied as part of the 'car's equipment'. However, there is no mention of this in the January 1951 edition. It is not known when this feature was withdrawn nor where on the car this spare quart can of oil was stowed (in the spare wheel compartment?).

Some cars have ammeter instruments calibrated to 20 amps whereas others have ammeters calibrated to 30 amps. The TD sports car's instrument calibrations were changed from 20 amp to 30 amp at car number TD 10779 (approximately at October 8, 1951). This would equate to Y-types up to Y 7045 having 20-amp instruments, whereas those few YAs following Y 7045 plus all the YBs would have had 30 amp instruments. It has not, however, been possible to confirm this theory definitely as yet.

Wing-to-body piping seems, in the main, to have been black (regardless of the colour of the individual car). This would seem to apply, at any rate, to all saloons. There is, however, in the Nuffield publication *News Exchange* of August 1949 a photo of what is clearly an Ivory coloured YT at the British Car Show in Montreal. It has light coloured (white or ivory?) wing-to-body piping.

Interior trim:
The erroneous rope-pull grab strap illustrations in the Y Workshop Manuals are of Morris fittings. However, the rope type of strap could be obtained from motor factors in the late 1940s and early 1950s and fitted separately later. When the Morris 10 Series M was reintroduced into production after World War 2 it was fitted with pillar loop grab straps instead of the prewar rope pulls. Where the interior of saloons was maroon, the grab straps apparently were maroon also.

There is a little evidence to suggest that a few green saloons had red (or, more properly, maroon) interiors. In June 1984 there was a 1947 YA for sale in Birmingham which was two-tone green and had a red interior. Likewise, there was also a 1947 YA for sale in London described as 'Almond Green with red interior'. Additionally, there is a car shown for sale in the January 7, 1949 issue of *The Autocar* also finished in green with a red interior and reported as first registered on October 1, 1947. It is *just* possible that all these cars had had their interiors exchanged for those from other cars.

As regards the YT, the pocket for the top bow of the hood has a zipper through the middle to cover the top bow. The welting was always the same colour as the interior regardless of the exterior colour of the car.

There is a 'for sale' advertisement in an issue of *Autosport* giving details of a new Y-type fitted with seat covers.

An Export Edition sales brochure for March 1950 gives 'brown' as an available interior upholstery colour for saloons. No evidence has, however, come to light to indicate that 'brown' was an actually available alternative to or a different shade from 'beige'; although both colours are shown as available in the text of the brochure.

The luggage straps in the boot were in all probability not fitted at the factory. The manual says, 'provision is made on the inside face of the boot lid for the fitting of luggage straps'. It seems to have been left up to individual owners to go to the trouble of fitting them. Those fitted to Y 5205 are leather with brass buckles (another University Motors addition?), whilst those on YB 1524 are made of webbing material. The majority of cars examined do not have any straps at all (and maybe were never, therefore, fitted with them by their owners).

APPENDIX 4

Alternative part numbers listings
by John Lawson & David Ransome

Electrical

Dynamo:

Lucas C39PV L-O 22250 (to XPAG/SC/14022)

Band cover	Lucas 227627	Remax ES976
Brush set	Lucas 227305	Remax CB405
Brush spring set	Lucas 228159	Remax ES1564
Commutator end bracket	Lucas 227594	Remax ES921
Commutator end bearing	Lucas 220258	Remax ES449
Drive end bracket	Lucas 227346	Remax ES928
Drive end bearing	Lucas 189307	
Armature	Lucas 227680	Remax ES725
Shaft nut	Lucas 180740	Remax ES940
Field coils	Lucas 227291	Remax ES395
Through bolt	Lucas 227269	Remax ES990
Oiler	Lucas 238367	Remax ES999

Austin A40 Devon; Bristol 401; Citroën Light 15; Hillman Minx Mk IV; Humber Hawk Mk IV; Jowett Javelin; Morgan Plus 4; Morris Minor; Morris Oxford MO; Morris Cowley; Riley RME; Land-Rover; Singer 9; Standard Vanguard; Triumph Renown & Mayflower; Vauxhall Wyvern & Velox; Wolseley 4/50; and many commercials.

Lucas C45Y V-3 (to XPAG/SC/16768):
(see YT Supplement for further details)

Lucas C39PV-2 L-O 22258 (to end of production)

Band cover	Lucas 227627	Remax ES976
Brush set	Lucas 227305	Remax CB405
Brush spring set	Lucas 228159	Remax ES1564
Commutator end bracket	Lucas 227702	
Commutator end bearing	Lucas 227713	Remax ES489
Drive end bracket	Lucas 227698	Remax ES929
Drive end bearing	Lucas 189307	
Armature	Lucas 227693	Remax ES843
Shaft nut	Lucas 180740	Remax ES940
Field coils	Lucas 227291	Remax ES395
Through bolt	Lucas 228336	
Oiler	Lucas 238367	Remax ES999

Austin A30, A40 Devon & Somerset; Bristol 401, 403; Citroën Light 15; Hillman Minx Mk IV, V, VI, Californian; Humber Hawk Mk IV & V; Jowett Javelin; Morgan Plus 4; Morris Minor; Morris Oxford MO, Cowley; Riley RME; Land-Rover; Singer 9; Standard Vanguard Phase I & II; Triumph Mayflower & Renown; Vauxhall E Series Wyvern & Velox; Wolseley 4/50, 4/44; and many commercials.

Starter motor:

Lucas M35G-1 L3-1 25022 (to XPAG/SC/14022)

Band cover	Lucas 250322	Remax ES975
Shaft cap	Lucas 250599	Remax ES1730
Brush set	Lucas 251108	Remax CB500
Commutator end bracket	Lucas 251104	Remax ES911

Commutator end bearing	Lucas 250626	Remax ES453
Brush spring set	Lucas 251109	Remax ES1591
Shaft nut	Lucas 250889	Remax ES937
Main spring	Lucas 250404	Remax SB16
Pinion & barrel	Lucas 250698	Remax SB43
Pinion retaining spring	Lucas 250691	Remax SB105
Drive end bracket	Lucas 250412	
Drive end bearing	Lucas 250678	Remax ES457
Armature	Lucas 250851	Remax ES749
Field coils	Lucas 251089	Remax ES772
Through bolt	Lucas 228066	Remax ES993

Austin A30, A40 Devon & Somerset; Hillman Minx Mk IV, V, VI, Californian; M.G. TD; Morris Minor; Singer 9; Triumph Mayflower; Vauxhall E Series Wyvern & Velox; Wolseley 4/44; and some commercials.

Lucas M418G AA80 25518 (to end of production)

Band cover	Lucas 255557	Remax ES981
Brush set	Lucas 255659	Remax CB370
Commutator end bracket	Lucas 256748	Remax ES907
Commutator end bearing	Lucas 255491	Remax ES465
Brush spring set	Lucas 238062	Remax ES1587
Location nut	Lucas 256482	Remax ES942
Drive assembly	Lucas 291353	
Sleeve & rubber	Lucas 291350	Remax SB64
Pinion & barrel	Lucas 291349	Remax SB66
Pinion retaining spring	Lucas 256027	Remax SB113
Drive end bracket	Lucas 256476	
Armature	Lucas 256575	
Field coils	Lucas 256578	Remax ES733
Through bolt	Lucas 256009	Remax ES995

Morris Six; Wolseley 6/80.

Steering column slip ring:
Lucas CSR4 L1 38254B (late type from Y 1261)

Starter switch (solenoid):
Lucas ST 764401 (to Y4459; push-button)
Remax ES1624
Lucas 76438B (push-button)
Lucas ST19/2 76423/764428 (to end of production; pull-type)
Remax ES1624、

Austin A30, A35; Morris Minor (early cars).

Distributor:
Lucas 40089 DKYH DA36 (all SC engines and to SC2/18096)
(only fitted to Y-type)
Lucas 40058F DKY 4A A131 (from XPAG/SC2/18097):
(only fitted to YB)
Lucas 40369 D2A4 DA43 (late YB)

Distributor Cap:
Lucas 409635 (all SC engines and to SC2/18096)
Remax ES1214 (all SC engines and to SC2/18096)
Remax Klearkap EST1214 (all SC engines and to SC2/18096)

Lucas 409563 (new no. DDB111) (from SC2/18097)
Remax ES1212A (from SC2/18097)
Remax Klearkap EST1212 (from SC2/18097)

Lucas 418888 (new no. DDB111) (late YB)
Remax ES1212A (from SC2/18097)
Remax Klearkap EST1212 (from SC2/18097)

DDB111 is still available from Lucas.

Distributor parts:

	40089	40058F	40369
Cap clip	410591	410591	418488
Brush & spring	404435	404435	418856
Rotor arm	400051	400051	400051 (new no. DRB101)*

Contact set	407C50	407050	407050 (new no. DSB122)*
Condenser	409613	409613	418113
Contact breaker	409614	409614	–
Cam	420588	420588	420068
Auto-advance:			
springs	406136/S	404598	420757
weights	400149	400149	418321
toggles	400141	400141	418707
shaft & plate	409580	409580	420672
Top bearing	404374	404374	–
Bottom bearing	410590	410590	419430
Clamping plate	404422	404422	–

DRB101: Approx 200 other applications. Still available from Lucas.
DSB122: Approx 150 other applications. Still available from Lucas.

Remax equivalents:

Brush & spring	CB331	CB331	CB335
Rotor arm	ES222	ES222	ES222
Contact set	ES79	ES79	ES79
Condenser	ES219	ES219	ES424
Contact breaker	ES219A	ES219A	–
Auto-advance:			
springs	ES1284	–	–
weights	ES1261	ES1261	–
toggles	ES1263	ES1263	–
Top bearing	ES492	ES492	–
Bottom bearing	ES491	ES491	–

Ignition Coil:
Lucas 45020 (new no.DLB101)
Remax ES2 Q12
Fixing bracket: Remax E1
(approx 500 other applications)

Suppressors:
Lucas WS5 78105 (not fitted until 1951)

Morris Oxford MO, Cowley, Six; Wolseley 4/50, 6/80.

Voltage control regulator:
Lucas RF 91   (to Y 0583)
Remax ES1956   (to Y 0583)

Lucas RF 95/2 L2 37065   (to YB 0325)
Remax ES1956   (to YB 0325)

Regulator	Lucas 33075	Remax ES1956A
Regulator cover	Lucas 334956	Remax ES1958
Cover clip	Lucas 334906	–
Resistance	Lucas 334977	Remax ES1959
Regulator contact	–	Remax ES299

Morris Oxford MO, Cowley; Wolseley 4/50; M.G. TD.

Lucas RB106/1 37138   (to end of production)
Remax ES1960   (to end of production)

Regulator	Lucas 33143	Remax ES1965
Regulator cover	Lucas 391600	Remax ES1962
Cover clip	Lucas 334906	–
Resistance	Lucas 334977	Remax ES1959

Morris MO; Wolseley 4/50; M.G. TD, TF, ZA, ZB, A, B (dynamo cars), Midget (dynamo cars), Magnette III & IV, 1100 & 1300 (dynamo cars); Austin Healey Sprite; BMC Farina range; BL Marina (very early cars only); BL Mini (dynamo cars); Austin A35; Riley 1.5, Elf; Wolseley 1500, Hornet; most, if not all, BMC and BL cars up to the introduction of the alternator.

Panel lights switch:
Lucas PS7 31201

Panel lights switch knob:
Lucas 314683

Panel light bulb holder:
Lucas 39007

Headlamps:
Lucas MBD 140	50458	(8in to Y4759)
Lucas S 700	50985	(7in all chrome; to Y7285 and from YB1240)
	50986	(7in; as above)
	51432	(7in chrome rim, shell painted as body colour of car; YB0251 to YB1239)
	50877	(Export; dip right)
	51016	(as above with

	50775	(Export USA)
		painted shell)
	51015	(Europe ex. France, with painted shell)

Headlamp parts:

	50458	50775	50985	50986
Rim	507577	553248	553248	553248
Lens	507586	–	–	–
Fixing wires	500291	504665	504665	504665
Rim screw	–	144291	144291	144291
Reflector	506855	553562	553935	553939
			553921	
Bulb holder	504801	859675	859696	859696
Fixing nut	180370	180370	180370	180370
Bulb	171	301	354	370

Headlamp parts (cont.):

	50877	51432	51015	51016
Rim	553248	554412	553248	553248
Lens	–	–	–	–
Fixing wires	504665	504665	504665	504665
Rim screw	144291	144291	144291	144291
Reflector	553562	553921	553939	553562
Bulb holder	554602	554602	859684	859684
Fixing nut	180370	180363	180370	180370
Bulb	301	354	370	301

BL Mini sealed beam units can replace YA, YT & YB 7in units.

Headlamp bulb holders: *Morris Minor.*

Fog lamp:
Lucas FT57 55010

AC; Daimler DB18; Triumph 2000 Roadster.

Lucas SFT575 55029

A70 Hereford; FX3 Taxi; Daimler DB18; Wolseley 4/50, 6/80.

Fog lamp parts:

	FT57 55010	SFT575 55029
Rim	532589	534343
Rim screw or catch	532590	144921
Lens	533597	–
Fixing wires	532997	504665
Gasket	533543	–
Reflector/Light unit	532588	552499

Adaptor/Bulb holder	532611	555001
Backshell	532584	–
Fixing nut	533537	180364
Junction box	770002	–
Base	504257	–
Bulb	87	185
Bracket	056117	056117

Fog lamp switch:
Lucas PS7 31201

Fog lamp switch knob:
Lucas 314683

Sidelamp:
Lucas 1130 52030

Sidelamp parts:
Rim	523937	Rim screw	118261
Bub holder	523964	Bulb	207

Stop/tail lamp
Lucas ST51/1 53027   (ST50 is similar)
Remax R352A (without dividing bar)

Tail/reverse lamp:
Lucas TR51/1 53032   (TR50 is similar)
Raydyot RT7

Stop/tail lamp parts:

	ST51/1 53027	TR51/1 53032
Fixing screw	524552	524552
Lens	522264 (Red)	521578 (Red/White)
	Remax LG33	LG330, LG33A
	524797 (N/Plate)	524797 (N/Plate)
Body	524776	524818
Bulb	207 & 57	207

Stop lamp switch:
Lucas 39C 31144
39C 31093 (LHD)

Dip switch:
Lucas FS22/1 31142
FS22/1 31284
360008A
Remax ES1631

Morris Minor; Morris Six MS, Oxford MO, Cowley; Wolseley 4/50, 6/80.

Reverse lamp switch:
Lucas 315500

Wolseley 4/50, 6/80.

Lucas 31077

Wolseley 4/50, 6/80.

Windscreen wiper motor:
Lucas CR4 CH28 75075
         CR2 DA36 072547
         CRT12 DA36 072821

Austin A30; Morris Minor (early cars);
Austin A35 Pick-up; Triumph TR2.

Windscreen wiper motor parts:

	CR4	CR2	CRT12
Motor	75075	75074	75144
Cover	738560	738560	741556
Brush gear	733661	733661	733661
Brush set	729367	729367	729367
Armature	736012	736012	739731
Field coils	734520	734520	739734
Guidewheel & plate	738905	738907	738907
Motor fixing parts	741628	741628	741628
Crosshead & rack	736010	736307	736307
Wheelbox/ control box	72564	72564	72564
Knob for above	736104	736104	736104
Grommet	734697	734697	734697

Windscreen wiper arms:
Lucas 735098: (early type, LH & RH)
         737596: (late type, LH)
         737595: (late type, RH)
Trico JLB-21C
Rex AA40-SS
Trico JSB-220C (early type)

Austin A30, A35, A40, A70; Citroën Light 15;
Ford Anglia & Prefect (1946-53); Humber Super
Snipe; Jowett Javelin; M.G. TF; Morris 8 Series E
(early type), Morris Minor (1951-56) (late type);
Riley 1½ Litre, 2½ Litre; Rover P4 (60 & 75);
Singer 10 & 12; Sunbeam Talbot 80, 90, Alpine;
Triumph Roadster, TR2, Renown.

Windscreen wiper blades:
Lucas 727707
         741543
         736414
         727802 (black)
         737681
Trico G500-8in C

Austin A30, A35; Morris 8 Series E; Morris
Minor.

Horns:
Lucas HF 1235 069344: (YA)
Raydyot EH12, EH16, EH14, EH17
Clearhooters HF 180, HF 500

Morris Cowley Van & J-type Van.

Lucas WT 614 69011: (YB Low Note)
               69012: (YB High Note)
Clearhooters C750A: (YB pair)

Morris Six MS, Oxford MO; Wolseley 4/50, 6/80,
1500; Riley 1.5; Austin A35.

Horn parts:

YA, YT:
Bracket 701639
YB:

Bracket	690617
Cover	702575
Contact set	702660 Remax ES1051
Diaphragm	702681
Resistance	702720

Horn relay:
Lucas 33116: (YB only)

Wolseley 4/50, 6/80; Jowett Jupiter.

Semaphore arms:
Lucas SF40N 54035
Tex B7C5

A40 Devon; Jowett Jupiter & Javelin; Morris
Minor (early cars); Sunbeam Talbot 90.

Lucas SF80 54044

A30, A40, Devon, A40 Somerset, A70 Hereford; Citroën Light 15; Humber Hawk Mk V, Super Snipe Mk IV; Jaguar Mk VII; Morris Minor, Oxford MO, Six MS, Cowley; Riley RME, RMF; Rover P4; Standard Vanguard Phase I & II; Sunbeam Alpine, Talbot 90; Triumph Mayflower; Wolseley 4/50, 6/80, 4/44.

Semaphore arm parts:

	SF40N 54035	SF80 54044
Arm	581175	582026
Cover	581124	582027
Lead	539698	582021
Bulb	256	256

Ignition switch:
Lucas S 312151
Lucas S45 31163

Interior light:
Wilmot-Breeden

Morris Oxford MO; Morris Oxford Srs II; Morris Cowley Srs II.

Interior light switch:
Wilmot-Breeden 8715/A

Lighting switch:
Lucas PPG1 31091

Morris Oxford MO; Morris Minor (early cars).

Switch knob:
Lucas 315002

Ignition warning light:
Lucas 318604

Ammeter:
Lucas CZU34 36028

Windscreen demister:
Lucas WH2 78005, 78005A

Fuse box:
Lucas SF6 033240 (YB only)

Wolseley 6/80, 4/50; Morris Minor.

Junction/terminal box:
Lucas 770069

Lucas 4J 78264
Cover: Lucas 77058

Wolseley 4/50.

Interior trim

Interior mirror:
Lucas 62011
Lucas 589/106 062581
      589/106A 062595
Desmo No.38
Eversure No.105
Tudor 55
Wingard 574A

Morris Minor (early cars)

Pedal rubbers:
Holdtite No.84

Morris 8 (1937/54), 10 (1946/54), 14 Cowley (1937/54), Wolseley 16, 21 (1946/54), 6/80, 4/40.

Dare PO21

Morris 8 Series E.

Centre arm rest mechanism:
(BL Marina range similar)

Interior door handles:
Wilmot-Breeden

Morris Oxford MO; Morris Commercial LD; Morris Cowley & Oxford Srs II.

Sunvisor brackets:
Wilmot-Breeden M1043/6

Morris Oxford MO; some 'Pay As You Enter' buses.

Windscreen winder handle:

Daimler DB18; Morris 8 Series E.

Grab straps:
Wilmot-Breeden

Daimler DB18.

Engine

XPJM (1,140cc) *Morris 10 Series M*

XPJW (1,140cc) *Wolseley 10*

XPAG (1,250cc) *M.G. TB, TC, TD, TF*

XPAW (1,250cc) *Wolseley 4/44*

Engine control link:

Morris Minor

Air filter canister:

Morris 12; Daimler DB18.

Air filter hose clamps:
Nesthill 575270 (2¾in diameter)

Head gasket & conversion set:
Payen HS1A532 (CS1A532): (to engine
SC2/17993)
  HS1A494 Mk1 (CS1A532): (from
SC2/17994)

Pistons:
Hepolite RS 8974

Piston rings:
Hepolite P4251 (x2)
  DO3576 (x2)
Cords Set No.20

Liners:
Hepolite FS1631

Valves & valve guides:
James 1988 & G1988 (inlet)
  1989 & G1989 (exhaust)
  K1988 (cotters)

Valve springs:
Terry's Aero VS349 (standard) (8 pairs)

VS481 (special) (8 pairs)
James 882 (inner), 883 (outer)

Engine bearings:
Glacier 22531/2 GS3204S M3041: (front &
rear mains)
  22533/4 GS3205S M3041:
(centre mains)
  3009 GS3046M B4163: (big
end)

Morris 10 Series M; Wolseley 10; Wolseley 4/44.

Vandervell: VP384? (mains)
  VP1436? (centre mains)
  VP1437? (front & rear mains)
  VP383? (big end)
  VP1255? (conrod)

Morris 10 Series M; Wolseley 10, 4/44.

Oil filter:
(From XPAG/SC2/17293)
Tecalemit Microfine FP3301
Tecalemit Felt FG2471 (or FG2381)
TJ FP3317
GP223
Purolator Micronic MF21A
Fram CH804PL
AC AC32A

Morris Oxford MO, Cowley.

(From XPAG/SC2/16916)
Fram PS821

Manifold gasket:
Payen 3473 or M3473: (all cars)

Exhaust flange gasket:
Payen 38T6 (to SC2/17993)
Payen 43T2 (from SC2/17994)

Sump gasket:
Payen SS9623 (to SC2/17993)
Payen SS9623 Mk I (from SC2/17994)

Valve cover gasket:
Payen 4633 (all cars)

Fiat 124 (with modification).

Timing chain:
Renold & Coventry 114038 (60 links; duplex):

Morris 10 Series M; Wolseley 10, 4/44; Morris Commercial PV, LC.

Spark plugs:
(To XPAG/SC2/17993)

Champion L-7 or L-10S
AC 45F
Bosch W145T1
Lodge C14; CN
KLG F50

(From XPAG/SC2/17994)
Champion N-8 or N-8B
AC 46XL
Bosch W145T2
Autolite AG5; AG7
Lodge CLNH
KLG FE50

Starter ring gear:
S93R   (to XPAG/SC/14022)
B120/10RS   (from XPAG/SC/14023)

Body and fittings

Bodyshell:

Morris 8 Series E; Wolseley 8.

SWC tool clips:

BMC Farina range.

SWC lid lock escutcheons:
Wilmot-Breeden M924/8

Morris Commercial LD (bonnet secured by three).

Bonnet catches and latches:

Morris 12 (without M.G. badge).

Bonnet top panels:

Morris 12.

Over-riders:

Ford Prefect (1946-53).

Doors and window glass:

Morris 8 Series E (4-door saloon).

Sunroof and windscreen:

Morris 8 Series E.

Door locator plate:
(saloon, rear doors):

Morris Minor.

Door hinge washers:

Austin A30, A35; Morris 8 Series E.

Bonnet corner rubbers:
Holdtite D815 (T Type; 90 degree angle)

Exterior door handles:
Wilmot-Breeden H480 (non-locking)

Austin A35 Van (locking; rear door handle less escutcheon); Morris Commercial LD (locking).

Wing and running board piping:

VW Beetle.

Boot lid handle:
Wilmot-Breeden 9423EXL

Austin A35.

Radiator blind:
Midland Wintershields 4302-T
Fabram 2558

Spare wheel compartment key:
Pennant 179
Wingard 768

Fuel system

SU H2 carburettor:
Morris Minor; Austin A35.

Petrol pump to carb flexible tubing:
Smiths Petro-flex PFP 27

Morris Minor (1953-56), 10, 12, 14 (1937-39).

SU electric fuel pump:

	SU	Remax
Cover	1466	ES1821B/104
Contacts	–	ES1822/102
Diaphragms	1697	ES1823A/504
Rocker/contact assembly	1438	ES1825/500
Bridge piece	–	ES1824/200
Rocker pin	1435	ES1826/1600
Diaphragm roller	–	ES1827/1600
Valve disc	839	ES1829/800
Inner valve housing washer	–	1830/800
Outer valve housing washer & strainer plug washer	1442	ES1831/800
Outlet union washer	405	ES1832/1000

Morris Minor (and many other applications).

Petrol tank sender unit:

MGA.

Transmission

Rear axle:

Wolseley 4/44; 15/50 (to car No 35857).

Propshaft universal joints:
Hardy Spicer K5-L1

Morris Oxford MO, Cowley; M.G. TD, TF, MGA, Magnette; Austin A30, A35, A40, A50, A55; Hillman Minx (1945-57), Husky (1955-57); Jowett Jupiter; Morris Minor 1000, Oxford Srs II; Singer 9, Gazelle (1956-57); Standard 8 & 10 (1953-57); Triumph Mayflower.

Speedometer drive cable:
Smiths/British Jaeger F243/52091

Clutch cover assembly:
Borg & Beck 45686/23 (7¼in, SC engines)

Morris Oxford MO; Austin A40; Nash Metropolitan; Hillman Minx Mk VII & VIII, Californian, New Minx Srs I, Husky; Triumph Mayflower.

Borg & Beck 45688/15 (8in, SC2 engines)

Morris Cowley Van & J-type; Austin A50 Cambridge, A55 Cambridge; Nash Metropolitan Srs III; M.G. TD, TF, ZA, MGA; Morris Oxford Srs II & III and Cowley; Sunbeam Rapier; Wolseley 4/44.

Clutch driven plate assembly:
Borg & Beck HB1316 45589/54 (7¼in, SC engines)

Morris Oxford MO; Austin A40; Nash Metropolitan; Minx Mk VII & VIII, Californian, New Minx Srs I, Husky; Jowett Javelin & Jupiter; Morris 10 Srs M; Sunbeam Talbot 80; Triumph Mayflower; Morris Minor.

Borg & Beck 47625/54 (8in, SC2 engines)

M.G. TD, TF, ZA, MGA.

Clutch release bearing assembly:
Borg & Beck 46892: (all cars)
Roadhog RH 2A: (all cars)

Many hundreds of applications to present day.

Clutch linings:
Ferodo VM2 B3/HI/2 (7¼in, SC engines)

Morris 10 Srs M; Singer Super 10 & Roadster; Vauxhall 10 & 12 (1940/48); Hillman Minx (1940/53).

Ferodo RYZ2 B1/VA/1 (8in, SC2 engines)

Bristol 2 Litre; Morris Oxford Mk II; Cowley Van; Vauxhall Velox & Cresta (1948/55)

Halfshafts:
Regent 720? (YA, YT and YB to YB0285)

Morris 10 Srs M?

Regent 1128? (from YB0286)

Wolseley 4/44?

Propshaft:
Hardy Spicer (tube length 36.625in – YA & YT)
Hardy Spicer (tube length 35.1875in – YB)

Gearbox bearings:
YB: (one of each except where specified otherwise)

	Ransome & Marles
Constant mesh pinion	LJ 1¼G(w/c)
Layshaft roller (x28)	N ⁵⁄₃₂in x 1in
Mainshaft (centre)	1/LJ 1⅛G
Mainshaft (rear)	LJ25
Selector steel balls (x18)	⁵⁄₁₆in
Mainshaft (x60)	N3 x 25mm
3rd speed gear (x18)	N3 x 28mm

BMC equivalent parts (these do not appear in the BMC-issue YB Parts List):

Mainshaft (rear)	11033
Selector (x18)	1279
Mainshaft (x60)	3839
3rd speed gear (x18)	14013

Steering

Steering wheel:

Morris Oxford MO; Morris Minor; M.G. TD, TF.

Tie rod ends:
Thompson TK57; KLJ71903

M.G. TF, ZA; Morris Minor MM, Series II; Wolseley 4/44.

Cooling system

Fan belt:

Ferodo V191

Mintex PK388; QT390
BTR/DonVee 223
John Bull 92
Goodyear 15
Romac C705
Raybestos R104

Fiat 1400; M.G. TC, TD, TF; Reliant Regal Mk V; Wolseley 4/44.

Water pump bearing:
Ransome & Marles 4/MJ12

Morris 10 Srs M, Oxford MO, Cowley, J-type Van; Wolseley 4/50, 6/80, 4/44.

Interior heater:
Smiths Universal R201
Tudor Twinfan 279, 280

Suspension

Hydraulic dampers:
Girling PVA6X (front, YB)
Girling PVA6 (rear, YB)
Luvax Girling PR5X/2 No. S.87/30 (front YA/YT)
Luvax Girling PPR5/7 LH No. S.87/31Y (rear YA/YT)
Luvax Girling PPR5/8 RH No. S.87/31X (rear YA/YT)

Rear springs
Duraflex 139106

Silentbloc bushes:
AAA629 (still available from BL/Unipart)

Rear spring rubber pads:
BL/Unipart ACG5232

Rear spring bush:
BL/Unipart ACA5242

Front suspension parts

Link, distance tube	(AAA 1322) (no. superceded by that below)
	BHH 1773 (Unipart)

Link, thrust washer	AAA 1390 (Unipart)
Link, seal	AAA 1323 (Unipart)
Link, support	AAA 1324 (Unipart)
Bottom wishbone assembly	AAA 1326 (Unipart)
Lower link bolt	AHH 4001 (Unipart)
Lower swivel pin bush	BTB 768
Bottom wishbone bush	AHH 7933
Upper swivel link (RH)	126895
Upper swivel link (LH)	126896
Lower swivel link (RH)	126897
Lower swivel link (LH)	126898

BMC Farina range; MGA; MGB; M.G. Z Magnette; M.G. Midget; Austin A30, A35, A40 (Farina); A40, A50, A55; Wolseley 15/50; Austin-Healey Sprite (Frogeye & later models).

Wheels:
Dunlop CDM 317

Wheel nuts:
BLMC 1800 range (same thread as YB)

Hubcaps (YB):

M.G. Z Magnette; M.G. 1100 & 1300; M.G. Magnette Mk III & IV; MGA.

Wheel trims:
Ace Turbo-Trim A2, C1, M19(RB) (15in wheels)		
Styla Sports Disc	SSD3	(16in sheels)
	SSD4	(16in wheels)
Styla Flyte Disc	SFD3	(15in wheels)
	SFD4	(16in wheels)
Styla Tyre Trims	STT4	(15in wheels)
	STT5	(16in wheels)
Styla Continental Disc	CD3	(15in wheels)
	CD4	(16in wheels)
Styla Spoke Disc	SPK3	(15in wheels)
	SPK4	(16in wheels)

Jackall hydraulic fluid reservoir:

Daimler DB18

Instruments

Speedometer:
British Jaeger Type SC52 Model 58597

Combined ammeter/oil pressure gauge/fuel gauge:
British Jaeger X58958 PA108

Oil seals

Front hub:
Payen C449

Morris Oxford MO, Cowley; Wolseley 4/50; M.G. TD.

Water pump seal:
Payen W110

Water pump front:
Payen 12404

Morris Oxford MO, Six MS, Cowley; Wolseley 4/50, 6/80; M.G. TD.

Water pump rear:
Payen 12185

Morris Oxford MO, Six MS, Cowley; Wolseley 4/50, 6/80; M.G. TD.

Gear box first motion shaft:
Payen B125:

Morris J-type Van

Gearbox mainshaft, rear:
Payen 12062

Pinion:
C451

Morris Oxford MO; Wolseley 4/50.

Rear hub, YB only:
Payen C450

Morris Oxford MO; Wolseley 4/50; Chrysler (UK) Avenger (timing cover oil seal).

Braking system

Brake master cylinder:
Lockheed NJ2 (YA & YT)
Lockheed NG1 (YB)

Morris Oxford MO, Six MS, Cowley; Wolseley 6/80, 4/50; Cooper 500cc & 1000cc; M.G. TD, TF; Morris Isis Srs II; Hindustan; Singer SM 1500, Hunter (1950s).

Master cylinder

parts:	NJ2	NG1
Assembly	22269	88187
Drain plug	8334	23558
Gasket	KL44532	KL44542
Cylinder barrel & tank	22268	25501
Filler plug	23894	89833
Gasket	KL46141	87240
Pushrod	incl with 22269	21413
Boot	437	437
Spring circlip	1012	KL47011
Stop washer	1002	1002
Secondary cup	400	87366 & 3008
Piston	429	21407
Piston washer	27979	90865
Main cup	112	588
Spring retainer	431	90839
Spring	3594	21410
Valve body	3589	2379
Valve cup	108128 & 608	108128 & 608
Valve washer	3590	27591
Valve assembly	3830	100795

Master cylinder repair kit:
Lockheed KL71410 (YA & YT)

Allard (1947/48), P1, P2, K2, K3, M2X, J2, J2X (1949/52); Alvis 3 Ltr, TC/108/G 3 Ltr; Armstrong-Siddeley 18hp (1951); Austin A125, A135, Princess III (1953/56); Bristol 400, 401, 402, 403, 404, 405, 407, 408 (1961/62); Frazer-Nash 2 Ltr Sports, Le Mans Mk II, Mille Miglia, Targa Florio (all models fitted with knock-on wheels only); Humber Super Snipe Mk IV, Pullman Mk II, Mk III, Mk IV, Imperial Mk I & II; Jaguar XK120, XK140; Lagonda 2½ Ltr Mk I, Mk II, 3 Ltr; Morris 10 Srs M, Srs II, Srs III, 12 Srs II, Srs III; Hindustan 10hp; Singer 9 Le Mans (1935), Drop Frame (1935), Sports (1935), 10hp (1938/48), 11 hp (1935/36), 12hp (1937/48); Sunbeam-Talbot 90; Wolseley Wasp & Hornet (1935), 14hp & 16hp Gazelle (1935), 6/90 Srs I, Srs II.

Lockheed KL71408 (YB)

Morris Oxford MO, Six MS, Cowley; Wolseley 4/50, 6/80; Austin Princess Mk IV (1956/62); Cooper 500cc & 1000cc; Hillman Minx Mk II, Mk III, Mk IV, Mk V, Mk VI, Mk VII, Mk VIII; Humber Hawk Mk III, Mk IV, Mk V, Mk VI; M.G. TD, TF; Morris Oxford Srs III (Manumatic); Hindustan; Morris Isis Srs II; Riley 2.6 Ltr; Singer SM1500, Hunter, Hunter S; Standard Vanguard Srs I; Sunbeam-Talbot 80, 90 Mk II, 90 Mk II, 90 Mk IIA; Sunbeam Mk III, Alpine Srs II; Triumph Mayflower, Renown; Vanden Plas Princess 4 Ltr; Wolseley 6/90 Srs III.

Front wheel cylinder:
Lockheed BA4 (YA & YT)

Morris 10 Srs M, 12 Srs III; Hindustan 10hp; Wolseley 10, 10 Srs III, 12 Srs III (rear), 12/48 Srs III (rear), 14/60 (rear), 14 Srs III (rear).

Lockheed BP3 (from YB0286, 2 per wheel)

Morris Oxford MO, Six MS, Cowley; Wolseley 6/80, 4/50; Cooper 500cc & 1000cc; Hillman Minx Mk III, IV, V, VI; Humber Hawk Mk III, IV, V; M.G. TD, TF; Singer SM1500, Hunter, Hunter S; Standard Vanguard Srs I, Srs II; Sunbeam-Talbot 90 Mk IIA; Triumph Mayflower, Renown; Wolseley 4/44, 15/50.

Front wheel cylinder repair kit:
Lockheed KL71429 (YA & YT)

Allard (1947/48); Humber 16hp, 18hp Snipe, Hawk (1946/47), Snipe 21hp, 18hp, Super Snipe (1940), Pullman Special, Pullman; Morris 10 Srs M, 12 Srs II, 10 Srs II & III, 12 Srs III; Hindustan 10hp; Singer 12hp & Super 12; Sunbeam-Talbot 14hp 2 Ltr, 3 Ltr, 4 Ltr; Wolseley 10, 10 Srs III, 14hp & 16hp Gazelle.

Lockheed 586 (from YB0286)

Morris Oxford MO, Six MS, Cowley; Wolseley 4/50, 6/80; Cooper 500cc & 1000cc; Hillman Minx Mk II, III, IV, V, VI; Humber Hawk Mk III, Mk IV, Mk V; M.G. TD, TF; Singer SM1500,

Hunter, Hunter S; Standard Vanguard Srs I, Srs II; Sunbeam-Talbot 80, 90 Mk IIA; Triumph Mayflower, Renown; Wolseley 4/44, 15/50.

Rear wheel cylinder:
Lockheed BA3 (YA & YT)

M.G. TC (front); Morris 10 Srs M, 12 Srs III, Hindustan 10; Wolseley 10, 10 Srs III.

Lockheed BX2 (from YB0286)

Morris Oxford MO, Six MS, Cowley; Wolseley 6/80, 4/50; Cooper 500cc & 1000cc; Hillman Minx Mk III, IV, V, VI; Humber Hawk Mk III, IV, V; M.G. TD; Singer SM1500; Standard Vanguard Srs I, Srs II; Sunbeam-Talbot 90 Mk II; Triumph Mayflower, Renown.

Rear wheel cylinder repair kit:
Lockheed KL71427 (YA & YT)

M.G. TA (front), TC (front); Morris 10 Srs M, 10 Srs II, 10 Srs III, 12 Srs II, 12 Srs III; Hindustan 10; Singer 9 Le Mans (front & rear), Drop Frame (front & rear), 11hp (front & rear), 12hp (front & rear); Wolseley Wasp & Hornet (1935), 10, 10 Srs III, 14hp & 16hp Gazelle.

Lockheed KL71469 (fromYB0286)

Morris Oxford MO, Six MS, Cowley; Wolseley 4/50, 6/80; Cooper 500cc & 1000cc; Hillman Minx Mk III, IV, V, VI; Humber Hawk Mk III, IV, V; M.G. TD; Morris Minor (early cars); Singer SM1500; Standard Vanguard Srs I; Sunbeam-Talbot 80, 90 Mk II, 90 Mk IIA; Triumph Mayflower, Renown; Wolseley 4/44.

Wheel cylinder parts:

	BA4	BA3	BP3	BX2
Assembly	9728	14579	30284	30285
Piston & dust cover	–	–	25277	36332
Cup	2762(x2)	131(x2)	586	586
Cup filler	–	–	29574	29574
Spring	2876	3869	29368	29368
Cylinder body	8154	14577	25300	25301
Handbrake lever	–	–	–	27785
Boot	5632(x2)	5107(x2)	–	27699
Piston – hydraulic	5644(x2)	6183(x2)	–	21692
Sealing ring	–	–	–	93858/14 & 36444/14

Pivot pin	–	–	–	36185
Bleeder screw	2286	12272	–	–
Crown spring	3865(x2)	3868(x2)	–	–

Morris Minor (some parts common to YB rear braking system)

Front flexible hose:
Lockheed KL49304 (YA & YT)
      or 12553
Lockheed KL57422/KL 48922 (LHD YT only)
Lockheed ML48804 (from YB0286)
      or KL56804, 57304, 101404

Morris Cowley, Six MS.

Rear flexible hose:
Lockheed KL49310 (YA & YT)
      or 12558
Lockheed KL57428/KL48928 (LHD YT only)
Lockheed KL48804 (from YB0286)
      or KL56804, 57304, 101404

Morris Oxford MO, Six MS; Wolseley 4/50.

Brake shoes:
Lockheed LB64 (YA & YT)

Lockheed LB34 (from YB0286)
Telamite TLS152 DL21 (from YB0286, shoe and lining set)

M.G. TD; Morris Cowley & Oxford Srs II; Wolseley 4/44, 1500.

Brake linings:
Ferodo Type MR19 BMO/27/3 (from YB0286)
Telamite TLS152 DL21 (from YB0286, shoe and lining set)

M.G. TD, TF; Morris Cowley & Oxford Srs II; Wolseley 4/50, 4/44 & 1500.

Ferodo Type MR19 BMO/27/1
  (YA, YT and YB to YB0285)

M.G. TB, TC; Morris 10 Srs II, III & M, 12 Srs III; Wolseley 10.

Handbrake cables:
Brivec BC250 (YA & YT o/s)
BC251 (YA & YT n/s)
BC252 (YB)

YT Supplement

Dynamo:
Lucas C45Y V/3 228334

Band cover	227015	Remax ES977
Brush set	203148	Remax CB364
Commutator end bracket	228195	
Commutator end bush	238567	Remax ES452
Oiler	238370	Remax ES999
Brush springs set	228159	Remax ES1564
Terminal cover	238234	Remax ES962
Drive end bearing	189308	
Drive end bracket	237119	
Shaft nut	180620	Remax ES935
Armature	228203	Remax ES711
Field coils	228075	Remax ES393

Starter:
Lucas M418G L-O 255378

Shaft cap	255780	Remax ES1732
Brushes	255659	Remax CB370
Commutator end bracket	255478	Remax ES906
Commutator end bearing	255491	Remax ES465
Contact set	255912	Remax ES1612
Brush springs set	270004	Remax ES1579
Shaft nut	255851	Remax ES938
Main spring	270889	Remax SB13
Pinion & sleeve	255649	Remax SB38
Pinion retaining spring	255728	Remax SB103
Drive end bracket	255073	Remax ES1317
Drive end brearing	270038	Remax ES466
Armature	255463	Remax ES744
Field coils	255625	Remax ES786

Starter switch:
Lucas ST19 L 764401; Remax ES1624

Adaptor plate:
Lucas DST1 764270

Switch coupling:
Lucas 764428

Distributor:
Lucas DKY4A   DA37   40162A

Plate	404442	
Cover	409563	Remax ES1212A & EST1212 (KK)
Brush & spring	404435	Remax CB331
Rotor arm	405468	Remax ES222
Contact set	407050	Remax ES79
Condenser	409613	Remax ES219
Cam	406329	
Auto advance springs	415486	
Auto advance weights	400147	Remax ES1261
Shaft & action plate	409579	
Top bearing bush	404374	Remax ES492
Bottom bearing bush	410590	Remax ES491

Ignition coil:
Lucas Q12 L 45020A
Remax ES2 Q12

HT Terminal nut	408120	
Fixing bracket Remax	E1	

Switchbox:
Lucas PLC6 L114 34018A

Ammeter:
Lucas BM4 L29 369269

Panel light switch:
Lucas PS6 L 314090

Warning light:
Lucas WL3/1 38013B

Warning light (headlamp beam):
Lucas WL4 318612 (USA only)

Foglamp switch:
Lucas PS6 L 314090

Panel connector:
Lucas 998390

Voltage control box:
Lucas RF95/2L 37057E
Remax ES1956

Cover assembly	334956	Remax ES1958
Clip	334906	
Resistance	334977	Remax ES1959

Headlamps:

Lucas S700	50821A	(LH home)
	50798A	(RH home)
	50821A	(Export)
	50775B	(USA)
Rim	553248	
Fixing wire	504665	

Light unit (for 50821A, 50798A) 552402
Light unit (for 50775B) 553562
Adaptor (for 50821A, 50798A & 50775B) 555005
Adaptor (for 50821A export) 858540
Bulb (for 50775B) 301
Bulb (for 50821A LHD) 300
Bulb (for 50798A) 162
Bulb (for 50821A RHD) 301

Fog lamp:
Lucas FT57 L1 55010A

Rim	532589
Glass	533533
Fixing wires	532997
Bead	532573
Reflector	532588
Bulb holder	532611
Backshell	532584
Fixing nut	533537
Bulb	87

Side Lamps:
Lucas 1130 52030A

Rim assembly	523937
Bulb holder	523964
Bulb	207

Lucas 1130 52134 (USA)

Rim assembly	523937
Bulb holder	552101
Contact mount	571576
Bulb	189

Stop/tail lamp:
Lucas ST51/1 53027B

Body	524776
Stop/tail glass	522264	Remax LG33
N/plate glass	524797	
Fixing spring	524763	
Fixing screw	524552	
Bulb	207	

Lucas 482/1 5313D (USA)

Glass	572507
Bulb	189

Reverse/tail lamp:
Lucas RT51/1 53032B

Stop lamp switch:

Lucas 39C DA36	31144A	(RHD)
Lucas 39C DA	31093A	(LHD)

Revese lamp switch:
Lucas SS10   315500

Dip switch:
Lucas FS22/1 L11 31142A

Cap	360026	(USA)

Flasher relays:
Lucas L1R 33095A (USA)

Horn push:
Lucas DA-8-47 32749E
Lucas DA-12-46 32726 (incl time switch, USA)

Steering column slip-ring
Lucas CSR4 L1 38254B

Slip-ring earth lead:
Lucas 858865

Steering column control:
Lucas DA/12/46 32726A

Choke control:

Lucas DA/10C/R48	32168B
Knob & wire assemby	325533
Body & tube assembly	325534

Starter control:

Lucas DA/10S/K48	32165B
Knob & wire assembly	329606
Body & tube assembly	325531

105

Screen wiper:
Lucas CW1 DA34 072545

Motor	730497
Brush set	730388
Armature	733108
RH wiper arm	732926
LH wiper arm	732927
Blade	727784
Bearing set	731721
Coupling bar	732191

Horns:
Lucas HF 1235 70036A

Bracket	701686

Lucas WT614 69011D (USA low note)
69012D (USA high note)

Bracket	702606
Cover	702575
Contact set	702660 Remax ES1051

Junction box
Lucas 4J 770069

Cable sets	RHD	LHD	USA
	859271	859273	859274
Main harness	976340	976340	976360
Panel harness	994191	–	994191
Starter leads	859267	859268	859268
	812406	812406	812406
	999706	999706	999706
	810811	810817	810817
Body harness	–	994211	–

Front flexible hose (brakes):
Lockheed KL57422
KL48922 (LHD cars only)

Rear flexible hose (brakes):
Lockheed KL57428
KL48928 (LHD cars only)

In compiling this listing every care has been taken to ensure accuracy. Neither the author nor the publishers, however, can be held responsible for any loss or damage resulting from the use of information contained in these alternative parts numbers listings. When purchasing parts for your car you should check all available reference sources before you buy.

LUBRICATION CHART, SERIES Y

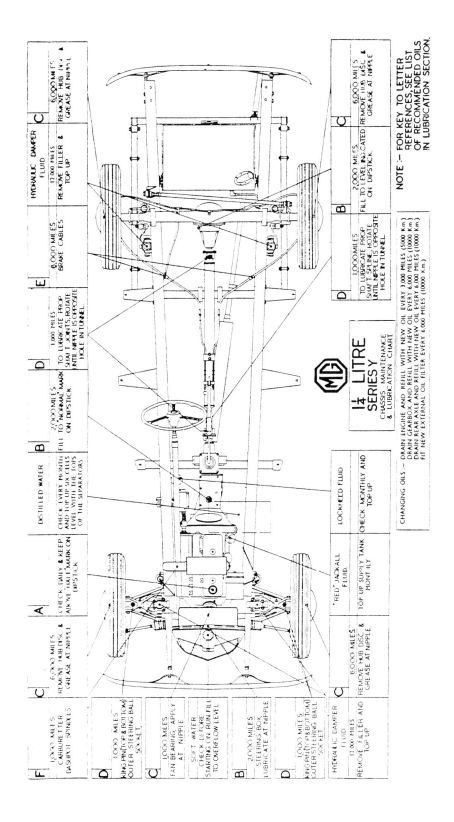

NOTE :- FOR KEY TO LETTER REFERENCES, SEE LIST OF RECOMMENDED OILS IN LUBRICATION SECTION.

CHANGING OILS :- DRAIN ENGINE AND REFILL WITH NEW OIL EVERY 3,000 MILES (5000 Km.)
DRAIN GEARBOX AND REFILL WITH NEW OIL EVERY 6,000 MILES (10000 Km.)
DRAIN REAR AXLE AND REFILL WITH NEW OIL EVERY 6,000 MILES (10000 Km.)
FIT NEW EXTERNAL OIL FILTER EVERY 6,000 MILES (10000 Km.)

MG 1¼ LITRE SERIES Y
CHASSIS MAINTENANCE & LUBRICATION CHART

THE M.G. 1¼ LITRE (Series "YB") LUBRICATION CHART

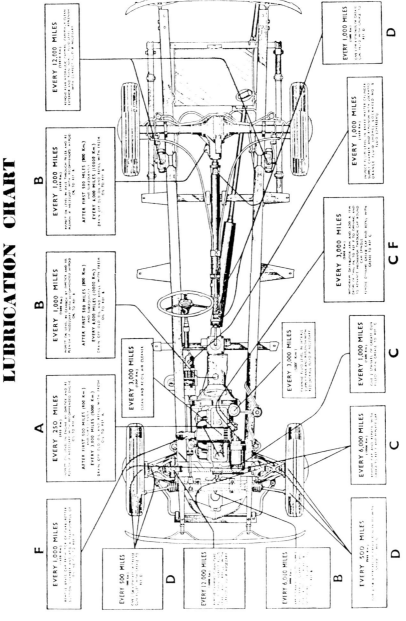

Every 1,000 Miles (1600 Km.). Use oilcan on all control joints, door locks and hinges to Ref. F.

The 1¼-litre M.G.

THE 1¼-litre engine used in the closed M.G. is identical with the well-known TC unit, but a single carburetter is fitted in place of the familiar twin S.U.s. It has a bore and stroke of 66.5 mm. and 90 mm. (1,250 c.c.), with a power-output of 46 b.h.p. at 4,800 r.p.m. Compression ratio is 7.2:7.4 to 1.

The engine assembly consists of a cast-iron cylinder block, integral with the upper half of the crankcase, aluminium-alloy sump-cum-bottom half of crankcase, cast-iron cylinder head, pressed steel o.h.v. cover and bolted on clutch housing is part of the block casting, whilst the lower is integral with the sump.

Both inlet and exhaust manifolds are independent castings, and there is no hot-spot provided. The entire engine-gearbox unit is flexibly mounted at three points, on rubber buffers.

Main engine components are disposed as follows: Nearside: dynamo, distributor, oil pump, dipstick and external oil filter. Offside: starter motor, manifolds and carburetter.

Inlet and exhaust valves are arranged in a single row down the centre of the head, they are inclined at an angle of 30 degrees from the vertical. The valves are actuated via rockers, push-rods and hollow guide blocks interposed between the camshaft and the base of the push-rods. The tops of the push-rods are cupped for the ball-ended, adjustable tappet screws.

The Aerolite, controlled-expansion alloy pistons have two compression rings and one slotted oil-control ring. The small ends of the con-rods are split and provided with a clamping bolt to secure the gudgeon pin which is rigidly held in the connecting rod and floats in the piston boss. The rods are of H-section steel with 45 mm. diameter big-end bearings of the "thinwall" type.

A twin sprocket is mounted on the front end of the statically and dynamically balanced, three-bearing (52.02 mm. diameter bearings) crankshaft, which drives the camshaft by Duplex roller chain. The oil pump is driven from a skew gear in the centre of the camshaft. A second skew gear is used for the distributor drive.

The nose of the crankshaft carries a pulley for the triangulated belt drive to the dynamo and the combined impeller and four-bladed fan assembly. A thermostat is interposed in the water outlet pipe, with a by-pass connecting direct to the water inlet.

Oil is drawn from the 1½-gallon sump via a gauze filter to the large gear-type pump, mounted externally on the cylinder block. The lubricant is filtered before circulation, first by the internal strainer, and then by an external filter of the "throwaway" type, immediately after passing the pump. Both pump and external filter are provided with relief valves; the first to deal with excessive pressures when lubricant is cold, and the second to by-pass oil if the filter itself becomes clogged. Normal pressure of the system is 50-70 lb. per sq. in.

From the filter the oil passes via an external pipe to an oil gallery running alongside the crankcase on the nearside. The gallery is connected by three passages communicating with the camshaft and crankshaft bearings. The first passage (nearest the front of the engine) leads to the front main bearing, and then to No. 1 big-end. It is worth noting that all big-ends have special oil holes drilled which coincide once in each revolution with a passage in the journal. The purpose of this is to inject a spurt of oil or to the cylinder walls, to supplement oil mist lubrication. Surplus oil from this lead is used to lubricate the timing chain.

The centre passage supplies the centre main bearing, the camshaft centre bearing, skew gearing and Nos. 2 and 3 big-ends. Finally, the rear passage leads to rear main bearing, rear camshaft bearing and then to No. 4 big-end.

Lubricant is taken to the overhead valve rocker shaft by an external pipe running from the gallery to a passage drilled in the cylinder head which registers with a hole in the rear rocker-shaft support. Oil drains back to the sump through the push-rod passages.

Crankcase pressure is relieved by a long breather pipe extending from the tappet inspection cover to the base of the engine.

Ignition is by Lucas 12-volt distributor (with automatic advance) and coil. Champion L.10 S sparking plugs are standardized.

A semi-downdraught single S.U. carburetter is used; attached to it is a horizontal, cylindrical combined air-cleaner and silencer of the oil-wetted type. Fuel is fed to the carburetter by an S.U. electric petrol pump. A Borg and Beck dry clutch is used.

Partly sectioned view of the 1¼-litre M.G. engine, by a staff artist of "The Light Car."

1947 CARS

The M.G. 1¼-litre Saloon

A New, Independently Sprung Model From a Famous Sports-car Factory

FEW cars made in this country have ever endeared themselves to so many enthusiastic drivers as has the M.G. Midget, which has been popular in different forms ever since 1928. Owners have always lamented the fact that, when growing families made an open two-seater unsuitable for them, they were obliged to buy a more touring make of car. Now the M.G. Car Co., Ltd., can offer them a four-seater saloon, powered by an engine of the same dimensions as the TC series Midget, combining comfort with a lively performance. The price of £671 11s. 8d., including purchase tax, exceeds that of the 2-seater model by only some 25 per cent.

The most striking innovation in the new 1¼-litre model is undoubtedly the adoption of independent springing for the front wheels. Eleven years ago the R type of racing M.G. Midget featured independent springing of all wheels, but only now have the manufacturers been sufficiently satisfied with their test results to incorporate independent suspension on a production model.

The potential gains from the elimination of a rigid front axle are very substantial. There can be some reduction in unsprung weight, to the advantage of both comfort and road holding. Flexible springs can be used without any wheel tramp or steering disturbances becoming troublesome. Braking stresses can be taken by rigid linkages, which ensure stability and control at all times. On the debit side of the balance sheet, however, it must be said that any system of I.F.S. needs

FAMILY LIKENESS.—The new model combines accepted M.G. lines with new standards of small-car comfort and refinement.

to be well designed and form part of a suitable chassis, otherwise these advantages may not materialize.

Hitherto the M.G. designers have held the view that cars with good orthodox suspension systems were better than cars with inadequately tested new layouts. During 1946 the first products of the Nuffield group of companies to use I.F.S. were announced, and the 1¼-litre M.G. follows this example. As a few observant motorists will be aware, the new design is anything but untried, having been in use on certain works cars throughout the war years.

Before details are described, a general picture of the style of the new car must be given. It is of a very popular size, in terms of both engine dimensions and body capacity. Rated at 11 h.p. by the now obsolete R.A.C. formula, the engine is of 1,250 c.c. swept volume, incurring an annual tax of £13.

In terms of body size, the 1¼-litre is a full four-seater, having very adequate enclosed luggage space. It provides this amount of accommodation within a wheelbase of 8 ft. 3 ins. and an overall length of 13 ft. 5 ins., so that it will fit into any normal garage. With no pretensions at being a large car, it does, nevertheless, display a very high standard of furnishing and general finish.

Any manufacturer introducing a new model at the present time faces a difficult choice in deciding the sort of body styling to adopt.

M.G. 1¼-LITRE SALOON DATA

Engine Dimensions:		Transmission— (Contd.)	
Cylinders	4	Prop. shaft	Hardy Spicer
Bore	66.5 mm.	Final drive	Spiral bevel
Stroke	90 mm.		
Cubic capacity ..	1,250 c.c.	**Chassis Details:**	
Piston area	21.5 sq. ins.	Brakes	Lockheed
Valves	O.H.V. push rod operated	Brake drum diameter	9 ins.
Compression ratio..	7.3/7.5	Friction lining area	90 sq. ins.
		Suspension, front ..	Independent, coil springs
Engine Performance:		Suspension, rear ..	Semi-elliptical
Max. b.h.p.	46	Shock absorbers ..	Luvax Girling
at ..	4,800 r.p.m.	Wheel type	Vent. disc
Max. b.m.e.p. ..	116	Tyre size	5.25 × 16.00
at ..	2,800 r.p.m.	Steering gear ..	Rack and pinion
B.H.P. per sq. in. piston area ..	1.82	Steering wheel ..	Spring spoke
Peak piston speed, ft. per min. ..	2,835	**Dimensions:**	
		Wheelbase	8 ft. 3 ins.
		Track, front	3 ft. 11¾ ins.
Engine Details:		Track, rear	4 ft. 2 ins.
Carburetter.. ..	Single S.U.	Overall length ..	13 ft. 5 ins.
Ignition	Coil	Overall width ..	4 ft. 10¼ ins..
Plugs: make and type	Champion L10.S.	Overall height ..	4 ft. 9 ins..
Fuel pump	S.U. electric	Ground clearance ..	6 ins.
Fuel capacity ..	8 gallons	Turning circle ..	35 ft.
Oil filter	Full flow	Dry weight	20 cwt.
Oil capacity	1½ gallons		
Cooling system ..	Fan and pump	**Performance Data:**	
Water capacity ..	13½ pints	Piston area, sq. ins. per ton	21.5
Electrical system ..	12 volt earth return	Brake lining area, sq. in. per ton ..	90
Battery capacity ..	51 amp. hr. (10 hr. rate)	Top gear m.p.h. per 1,000 r.p.m. ..	14.6
		Top gear m.p.h. at 2,500 ft./min. piston speed ..	61.8
Transmission:		Litres per ton-mile, dry	2,570
Clutch	Borg and Beck 7 in.		
Gear ratios	Top 5.143		
	3rd 7.121		
	2nd 10.646		
	1st 18.000		
	Rev. 18.000		

PROPORTION.—Fitting a comfortable four-seater saloon body on a chassis of only 8 ft. 3 in. wheelbase, the M.G. stylists have contrived to give the car excellently balanced lines.

The M.G. 1¼-litre Saloon—Contd.

Many present-day foreign cars, from the continents of both America and Europe, favour flowing, even bulbous, lines, with every possible part recessed into the body panelling. In England, however, there is a very strong body of opinion which adheres to the more classic line— the car which may be said to " look like a car."

The model now described represents an unhesitating affirmation of the orthodox school of thought. It is a typical four-door, six-light saloon, with luggage boot, and although its lines are more flowing than those of previous M.G. saloons, it represents the modern development of a theme rather than any break with tradition.

The foundation of the car is a chassis of generally orthodox layout, but good design has produced a notable combination of lightness and rigidity. The main side members are formed from inward facing channels, with shallow channel members welded in to form torsionally rigid boxes. With adequate main members, and some support from a steel saloon body, elaborate cross bracing can often be dispensed with; in this case, a box-section cross member carries the front suspension system, and tubular bracing members are located under the gearbox, ahead of the rear axle, and at the extreme rear of the frame.

The independent front wheel springing system is, basically, of a type which has been used on certain American and Continental touring cars for almost 15 years, a period which has shown the principle to be sound but good detail design vital. Each wheel is located by a pair of transverse wishbone-shaped links, the lower member slightly the longer of the two, the geometry of the linkage being such that the wheel can rise or fall against a coil spring without changes in track or wheel camber of serious magnitude arising.

The behaviour of such a system when the car is new depends on a good geometrical layout and on mechanical parts being stiff enough to prevent undesirable deflections under any loading conditions. Proof of the correctness of the M.G. design was obtained when we covered substantial mileages in a prototype car, both in England and abroad, early this year.

For sustained good behaviour throughout the life of a car, all the bearings in a suspension system must remain free from backlash, even if somewhat neglected. An I.F.S. system must almost inevitably comprise a number of highly loaded joints, and these need careful designing.

In the system here described, rubber bushes are provided for the bearings securing the wishbone members to the chassis. Such bearings need no lubrication, and, being widely spaced, can safely be made slightly flexible—whereby the car is quietened. For the outboard bearings, however, plain bushes with grease-nipple lubrication are used. The kingpin bearings are an unusual feature of the design, orthodox thrust races being superseded by a threaded construction which gives a very large bearing surface. The sliding thread surfaces are lubricated from the wishbone bearing nipples, and only require attention at very infrequent intervals.

Rear suspension is by a rigid axle and half-elliptic leaf springs. Here, as elsewhere, the design is orthodox in principle, but clever in detail. The flexible seven-leaf springs, for example, have rubber inserts between the leaves, and are shackled directly on to extensions of the tubular chassis cross members, the frame being swept downwards slightly to pass below the axle. An unusual feature is the provision of a rubber-mounted sway-eliminator rod, linking the offside frame member to the nearside of the axle casing.

In keeping with the comprehensive standard of equipment which distinguishes the model is the fitting of Smith's Jackall permanent jacks. This is a hydraulic system, and by operating a hand pump under the bonnet either the front or rear of the car may be lifted, with a minimum of effort and with no soiling of hands or clothes. The actual jack units are mounted on the chassis frame at the front of the car, and at the rear on the axle tube between springs and chassis frame.

Pressed-steel wheels of five-stud pattern are used, slots near the rim providing ventilation for the brakes and allowing snow grip chains to be fitted. Lockheed hydraulic brakes with 9-in. diameter drums are applied to all wheels, and a hand lever between the front seats applies the rear brakes through the medium of flexible cables. This parking brake is adjustable from inside the car.

A rack and pinion steering mechanism has been adopted, an almost frictionless gear being satisfactory with a good independent springing system. Mounted ahead of the front hubs, the rack controls the wheels through the medium of two short track-rod sections, the layout combining freedom from interaction between springing and steering with the minimum number of joints. A pre-loaded spring controls the meshing of the

WALNUT FACIA.—The use of good quality wood gives an unusually pleasant interior, instrument faces perpetuating the M.G. octagon motif.

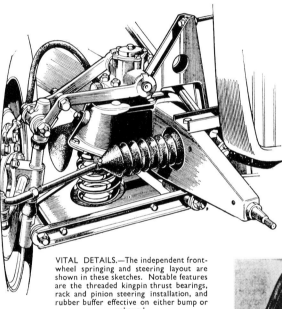

VITAL DETAILS.—The independent front-wheel springing and steering layout are shown in these sketches. Notable features are the threaded kingpin thrust bearings, rack and pinion steering installation, and rubber buffer effective on either bump or rebound.

rack and pinion, and a rubber-bushed universal joint is incorporated in the steering column.

The engine of the new car is fundamentally similar to the well-tried unit fitted to Midget series TC cars. It differs somewhat in respect of accessory mountings, however, has a slightly different camshaft to produce the discreet silence and flexibility becoming to a saloon car, and is fed with mixture by a single S.U. carburetter.

This engine is well suited to the capacity taxation system which came into force on January 1, the stroke/bore ratio of 1.35 being low enough to combine generous piston area with moderate tax. A counterbalanced crankshaft mounted

in three thin-wall bearings, in conjunction with rigid connecting rods and big-end bearings of similar type, provide the foundation for a very sturdy power unit which should withstand long periods of hard use. Push-rod-operated overhead valves, of generous size and inclined at a small angle to the vertical, combine with well-shaped ports to make possible a very good power output.

Typical of the care which has gone into details of the engine is the special provision made to prevent oil passing down the overhead-valve guides. Any tendency for oil consumption to increase during the life of the car owing to wear of the valve guides is checked by

FINE FURNISHING.—Leather upholstery and comprehensive equipment provide the amenities for extremely pleasant travel.

The M.G. 1¼-litre Saloon—Contd.

special oil seals—a double advantage is secured from these seals, in fact, for their presence permits the valve gear to be fed with unusually generous quantities of oil, so reducing the probable rate of wear.

In terms of cold figures, the best pulling power of the 1¼-litre engine corresponds to 116 lb. per sq. in. brake mean effective pressure, at a speed of 2,800 r.p.m., promising really good acceleration at around 40 m.p h. in top gear. Maximum power output is of slightly less importance in a saloon model, since few drivers use maximum revs. in the gears when handling this type of car, but an output of more than four times the rated horse power is usefully above the average.

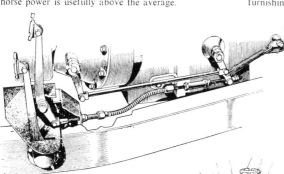

INCONSPICUOUS REFINEMENTS.— Shown above is the clutch control mechanism, combining accessibility for adjustment with freedom from interference by engine movement. On the right is the rear axle, with rubber-insulated transverse stabilizer rod, interleaved semi-elliptic springs, and dual flexible hydraulic pipelines to brakes and jacks.

In conjunction with this engine, a single dry-plate Borg and Beck clutch is used, a four-speed gearbox completing the power unit assembly. Synchromesh engagement is provided for top, third and second gears, and the indirect ratios are high enough to permit the attainment of usefully high speeds in accordance with the tastes of enthusiastic drivers. The need for a remote gear control has been overcome by locating the selector mechanism at the rear of the gearbox, a short gear lever with very modest movement coming readily to hand.

An open tubular Hardy Spicer propeller shaft is used, with needle roller bearing universal joints. The length of this shaft is reduced, to the advantage of smooth running at high speeds, by an extension of the gearbox tailshaft. To keep the exhaust system well clear of the low floor of the car, without sacrifice of ground clearance, the silencer has been given an unusual location directly below the propeller shaft.

The complete power unit is mounted on vibration-absorbing rubber pads, under the nose of the engine and under the rear of the gearbox. These rubber mountings are supplemented by a transverse rod which holds the power unit at the level of its centre of mass—thus the unit can rock to absorb the inevitable torque irregularity of a four-cylinder engine, but cannot move about bodily.

A clever detail is the clutch-operating linkage. A flexible cable in tension links the frame-mounted clutch pedal to an arm pivoted near the front of the engine, via an accessible threaded adjustment. From this lever a push-rod runs back to the actual clutch-withdrawal

mechanism. This design provides a clutch control unaffected by movement of the engine on its rubber cushions, and also convenient adjustment of clutch pedal clearance.

Sturdy pressed-steel saloon bodywork is fitted to the new model, providing useful extra stiffening for the box-section chassis frame. At the front, tubular chassis bracing members extend downwards and forwards from the dashboard structure to give the utmost rigidity of the front end assembly. Seen under construction, the generous use of sound-damping material on body panels is noted.

Four doors of adequate size give access to the body, revealing an exceptionally high standard of interior furnishing. Individual leather-upholstered front seats are comfortably wide, yet give some of the lateral support provided by sports car bucket seats. The rear seat has side armrests and a folding central armrest, providing very comfortable travel for two people.

Walnut has been freely used for the interior of the body, notably, door fillets and the instrument board. The usual speedometer, clock, oil-pressure gauge, fuel-contents indicator, and ammeter face the driver, a roomy locker occupying the opposite half of the facia panel. A telescopic steering column is provided, with wing-nut clamp, carrying a simple three-spoke spring wheel. Trafficators are controlled from a knurled ring on the steering-wheel hub, and are self-cancelling under the influence of a time switch. Lighting switchgear is unusual, in that a dashboard knob is pulled for side lamps, then twisted and pulled again to bring the head lamps into operation. Stop lamp, reversing lamp, and a powerful fog lamp form part of the car's standard equipment, as do such other all-condition items as rear blind, sun visors, a sliding roof and an opening windscreen.

A capacious luggage locker provides for all normal requirements. When large amounts of baggage have to be carried, however, the lid of this locker can be left open to form a flat extension of the floor. Underneath the luggage locker is a separate compartment housing the spare wheel and tools, the lid of which incorporates the lamps and number plate—these remain lighted and visible even when the compartment is open.

The 1¼-litre M.G. is a highly developed small car which promises to combine comfort and good detail finish with a very brisk road performance. Cars have been in production at the Abingdon-on-Thames factory for some time past, and examples are already in the hands of M.G. distributors as far afield as India, Australia and South America.

The Motor Continental Road Test No. 1c/47—

Make: M.G.   **Type:** 1¼-litre Saloon

Makers: The M.G. Car Co. Ltd., Abingdon-on-Thames, Berks.

Dimensions and Seating

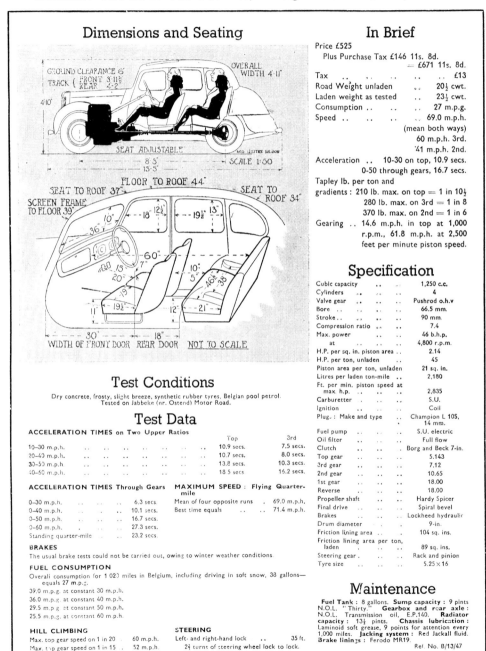

In Brief

Price £525
  Plus Purchase Tax £146 11s. 8d.
      = £671 11s. 8d.
Tax £13
Road Weight unladen .. 20½ cwt.
Laden weight as tested .. 23½ cwt.
Consumption .. .. .. 27 m.p.g.
Speed .. .. 69.0 m.p.h.
      (mean both ways)
      60 m.p.h. 3rd.
      41 m.p.h. 2nd.
Acceleration .. 10-30 on top, 10.9 secs.
      0-50 through gears, 16.7 secs.
Tapley lb. per ton and
gradients : 210 lb. max. on top = 1 in 10½
      280 lb. max. on 3rd = 1 in 8
      370 lb. max. on 2nd = 1 in 6
Gearing .. 14.6 m.p.h. in top at 1,000
      r.p.m., 61.8 m.p.h. at 2,500
      feet per minute piston speed.

Specification

Cubic capacity	.. ..	1,250 c.c.
Cylinders	.. .. ..	4
Valve gear	.. .. ..	Pushrod o.h.v
Bore	.. .. ..	66.5 mm.
Stroke	.. .. ..	90 mm.
Compression ratio	.. ..	7.4
Max. power	.. ..	46 b.h.p.
at	.. ..	4,800 r.p.m.
H.P. per sq. in. piston area	..	2.14
H.P. per ton, unladen	..	45
Piston area per ton, unladen		21 sq. in.
Litres per laden ton-mile	..	2,180
Ft. per min. piston speed at max. h.p.		2,835
Carburetter	.. ..	S.U.
Ignition	.. ..	Coil
Plug : Make and type	..	Champion L 10S, 14 mm.
Fuel pump	.. ..	S.U. electric
Oil filter	.. ..	Full flow
Clutch	.. ..	Borg and Beck 7-in.
Top gear	.. ..	5.143
3rd gear	.. ..	7.12
2nd gear	.. ..	10.65
1st gear	.. ..	18.00
Reverse	.. ..	18.00
Propeller shaft	.. ..	Hardy Spicer
Final drive	.. ..	Spiral bevel
Brakes	.. ..	Lockheed hydraulic
Drum diameter	.. ..	9-in.
Friction lining area	..	104 sq. ins.
Friction lining area per ton, laden		89 sq. ins.
Steering gear	.. ..	Rack and pinion
Tyre size	.. ..	5.25 × 16

Test Conditions

Dry concrete, frosty, slight breeze, synthetic rubber tyres, Belgian pool petrol.
Tested on Jabbeke (nr. Ostend) Motor Road.

Test Data

ACCELERATION TIMES on Two Upper Ratios

	Top	3rd
10–30 m.p.h.	10.9 secs.	7.5 secs.
20–40 m.p.h.	10.7 secs.	8.0 secs.
30–50 m.p.h.	13.8 secs.	10.3 secs.
40–60 m.p.h.	18.5 secs.	15.2 secs.

ACCELERATION TIMES Through Gears

0–30 m.p.h.	6.3 secs.
0–40 m.p.h.	10.1 secs.
0–50 m.p.h.	16.7 secs.
0–60 m.p.h.	27.3 secs.
Standing quarter-mile	23.2 secs.

MAXIMUM SPEED : Flying Quarter-mile

Mean of four opposite runs .	69.0 m.p.h.
Best time equals	71.4 m.p.h.

BRAKES

The usual brake tests could not be carried out, owing to winter weather conditions.

FUEL CONSUMPTION

Overall consumption for 1,020 miles in Belgium, including driving in soft snow, 38 gallons—equals 27 m.p.g.

39.0 m.p.g. at constant 30 m.p.h.
36.0 m.p.g. at constant 40 m.p.h.
29.5 m.p.g. at constant 50 m.p.h.
25.5 m.p.g. at constant 60 m.p.h.

HILL CLIMBING

Max. top gear speed on 1 in 20   60 m.p.h.
Max. top gear speed on 1 in 15 .   52 m.p.h.

STEERING

Left- and right-hand lock .. .. 35 ft.
2¾ turns of steering wheel lock to lock.

Maintenance

Fuel Tank : 8 gallons. **Sump capacity :** 9 pints N.O.L. "Thirty." **Gearbox and rear axle :** N.O.L. Transmission oil, E.P.140. **Radiator capacity :** 13½ pints. **Chassis lubrication :** Laminoid soft grease, 9 points for attention every 1,000 miles. **Jacking system :** Red Jackall fluid. **Brake linings :** Ferodo MR19.

Ref. No. B/13/47.

————THE M.G. 1¼-LITRE SALOON

A Well-equipped Small Car Coupling High Quality and Refinement with Brisk Performance

AMONG the unique products of the British motor industry is a group of cars which, despite small size, are of extremely high quality. Costing, perhaps, almost twice as much as the cheapest makes of comparable size, such models offer a high standard of refinement and performance, together with the usual small car advantages of compactness and economical running.

A new-comer to this field, even though it is in some ways the lineal descendant of a rather larger 1939 model, the 1¼-litre M.G. promises to become an enduring favourite. Casual examination shows it to be an appealing little car, smart and well equipped; a road test of unusually comprehensive extent, carried out some months ago on an early production car, convinced us that appearances do less than justice to a mechanically excellent design.

Our road test of the 1¼-litre M.G. covered the customary distance on English roads, some 700 miles in the hands of different drivers. Supplementing this, we have had experience of more than 1,000 miles over the roads of Belgium and Luxembourg in the same car.

Reversing the chronological order of tests, it is interesting to record, first, the outline of our Continental experiences with the car. Leaving the quayside at Ostend, a local courier in the back seat began by giving directions how to avoid the bumpiest pieces of cobbled road, then lapsed into silence, and finally remarked: " a very comfortable car, this." In the course of 1,000 miles, many of them over snow, the M.G. received no maintenance and developed no squeaks or rattles, consumed only a pint of oil, and was never touched with a tool, except when one punctured tyre was changed. At the end of the trip, a speed of 70 m.p.h. was held for many miles along the Jabbeke motor road, a speed actually above the normal maximum, without the car showing any signs of distress.

It must be emphasized that, although the octagonal radiator badge is generally associated with racing and sports cars, the 1¼-litre M.G. should rather be regarded as a refined fast touring car. The figures printed on the opposite page leave no doubt that, in terms of acceleration and maximum speed, the car has a performance which is well above the average. Nevertheless, its real function is the daily chores of a four-seater saloon, tasks which it performs briskly with extreme comfort for driver and passengers.

The four-door body of the 1¼-litre M.G. has been designed on conservative lines. The car is a typical, good-looking British sports saloon, making no concessions to transatlantic styling trends. It is a comfortable body, however, easily entered and easy to see out of. "Armchair comfort" is the only phrase for the leather-upholstered seats, the front ones being luxurious, yet shaped to eliminate side sway, while the rear seat has a folding central armrest. The luggage boot is quite capacious, as was verified abroad, easily accommodating a large suitcase, spare fuel can, and miscellaneous packages, without the flat-folding lid needing to be left open.

Driving Comfort

A driver entering the car is immediately put at his ease by conveniently placed controls and excellent forward vision. The orthodox seat adjustment is supplemented by a telescopic steering column, the pedals are so spaced that the largest foot need never depress two simultaneously or rest upon the clutch, and a short gear lever is convenient to the left hand. A neat instrument panel faces the driver, equipped with speedometer, clock, fuel contents gauge, oil-pressure gauge and ammeter, neat push-pull switches operating starter, fog lamp, dash lamp, head and side lamps.

Driving away, one quickly becomes charmed by a very delightful car. Mechanical noise inside the car is generally very slight, and the riding on cobbled city streets is extremely comfortable. The steering is extremely light, and not unreasonably low-geared.

On the open road there is an initial impression that the car's performance is relatively indifferent, for one receives no sensations of speed or fierce acceleration. One soon discovers, though, that each time a traffic signal changes from red to green the M.G. moves smartly to the head of the bunch, and stays there, a phenomenon which recurs so regularly that it eventually has to be attributed to inconspicuously rapid acceleration by the M.G. rather than to loitering by other drivers.

When the performance of the car is checked by stop-watch and Tapley meter, there is yet more surprise, for, in terms of both speed and acceleration, the figures obtained are outstanding for a luxurious 11 h.p. saloon. Only a breath of tail wind is necessary for the car to attain an honest 70 m.p.h. on the level, a speed at which the speedometer of the car tested showed an error of less than 5 m.p.h.

The 1¼-litre M.G. Saloon—Contd.

Acceleration and hill-climbing abilities of the 1¼-litre M.G. like its speed potentialities, are inconspicuous until they are checked on well-known hills. In top gear, the engine pulls most effectively at around 35 m.p.h., but even though the performance falls off below this speed and becomes less regular below 20 m.p.h. the acceleration figure between 10 and 30 m.p.h. on top gear is extremely creditable. On known hills, the car maintains unexpectedly high speeds, pinking slightly on Pool petrol, but otherwise giving no sign that it is working hard.

The rack-and-pinion steering of the 1¼-litre M.G. is in the best race-bred tradition, absolutely positive and free from play, yet extremely light. It is without doubt steering which will delight the keen driver. The car as a whole displays a marked oversteering characteristic, so that its cornering is really willing, and calls for the minimum of wheel movement. The concomitant of this willingness to take corners is, almost inevitably, that the car requires attention from the driver when it is being driven at maximum speed, particularly if the tyre pressures are low, to avoid a slight snaking tendency.

The M.G. can be driven extremely fast over rough roads, the coil-spring I.F.S. system and flexible but well-damped rear suspension combining to smooth out either individual bumps or corrugated surfaces. There is a pleasant lack of any thudding, or of body squeaks and rattles, symptoms of distress which some cars give, even though they are riding fairly comfortably. On rough, cobbled Belgian main roads tackled at speed, the light, frictionless steering allowed a fair amount of reaction to reach the driver's hands, but there is never any question of large movements of the spring steering wheel.

Slippery roads haunted us during our tests in England and abroad, and the fiercest types of cornering could seldom be indulged in. Nevertheless, we formed the impression that, despite a moderate degree of roll, the M.G. cornered well, any slides which were provoked proving instantly controllable. Fast and bumpy corners were tackled, carrying two people and much luggage, without the springs ever bottoming.

Starting from cold proved extremely good, even though the car was left standing out in a snowstorm overnight. Although the full performance was not obtainable until the engine warmed up, the car pulled steadily without use of the choke almost immediately after starting. Obviously, carburetter settings on the test car were not unduly weak, yet the recorded fuel-consumption figures were eminently satisfactory.

Our test gave us little chance to test accessibility, since it was entirely trouble-free. The two grease nipples on the king-pins were lubricated before the car was taken abroad, and after 1,300 miles there was no steering stiffness or other sign of maintenance being needed. The car used no water during the test, and had a negligible oil consumption.

One puncture showed the permanent jacks to work well, waggling of an under-bonnet lever raising the car into the air; it must be admitted, though, that with memories of earlier M.G. cars we shed a tear for the unenclosed spare wheels and centre-lock hubs of days past.

Brakes on the 1¼-litre M.G. are Lockheed hydraulic, of a size adequate for the car. No more need be said concerning their smooth effectiveness, except to add that the hand brake, located between the front seats, is also entirely up to its job.

The Borg and Beck clutch on the new car takes up the drive smoothly, yet only slips momentarily when gear-changing methods which are, frankly, wicked, are tried out. The gearbox is delightful, with good synchromesh mechanism which does not interfere with old-fashioned methods of gear-changing. Sporting drivers will appreciate the quick changes of ratio; for example, it is possible to trickle gently through traffic in top gear, yet, when opportunity arises, change instantly and directly into second gear for really fierce acceleration.

One of the worries which besets road testers is the fact that cars in catalogued condition are prone to lack important aids to pleasant travel; too frequently

The interior furnishing of the car is in accordance with the best British standards, with leather upholstery, walnut facia panel, neat instruments and accessible controls.

one can become trapped far from home in a car which lacks such "non-essentials" as a fog lamp. Full marks go to the M.G. on this score, for it carries as standard equipment fog lamp, reversing lamp, opening windscreen, and all the vital accessories to year-round driving.

In sum, we feel that the M.G. 1¼-litre is an extremely creditable car, a model which we would unhesitatingly order for personal use. Conservative in appearance, it offers good performance and the benefits of a modern design of chassis. It is a car which promises to prove justly popular, both in Britain and abroad, for many years to come.

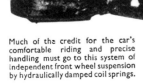

Much of the credit for the car's comfortable riding and precise handling must go to this system of independent front wheel suspension by hydraulically damped coil springs.

An Open "1¼"

M.G.'s Introduce New Tourer Body on Well-tried Chassis

The ease and tidiness with which the hood is stowed away are emphasized in this view of the M.G. in its role as an open car. The windscreen can fold flat on to the bonnet.

A NEW arrival from the M.G. stable is the 1¼-litre open tourer. It is designed for the export market, and in particular America, and there are no prospects of delivery at the moment in this country. The basis of the tourer is the same chassis as that for the saloon with the following main modifications:

1. The steering is left hand and the pedals have been adjusted accordingly. The gear lever and hand brake retain their central position.

2. The battery box on the engine bulkhead has been moved to a central position and the engine oil pump has been modified to clear the steering column. Important new features are the TC camshaft and twin S.U. semi-downdraught carburettors, which give the engine a distinct resemblance to that of the Midget.

Plenty of Light

The hood, which, as can be seen from the illustration, is both serviceable and good-looking, has unusually large window space and appears to have been well designed to combat draughts. It stows away neatly when not being used, without causing inconvenience to the passengers.

As regards the driver, the telescopic steering wheel enables even those above average height to drive in comfort. The front seats, which move smoothly and easily, hinge forward to enable back seat passengers to enter.

The instruments are easy to read from the driving seat and in size and in detail are similar to those on the saloon. In the centre of the steering wheel are the horn and the operating switch for the traffic signals, a knurled disc which operates the twin tail lamps and the double-filament bulbs in the side lamps in a special manner detailed below to conform with requirements in the U.S. Otherwise its operation is the same as in the 1¼-litre saloon, working on a time basis. There is also an indicating light to the left of the driver which goes on only when the head lights are on but not dipped, thus obviating a great deal of annoyance and danger to other road users.

The dipping switch is on the floor to the left of the driver and sufficient space is provided for the left foot without causing the foot to be cramped or uncomfortable during a long drive. The mirror is of a reasonable size and well placed to get a clear view. A rear blind is not fitted. The same generous

luggage space that is a feature of the saloon has also been allotted on the tourer. Close by is the petrol tank with a capacity of 8 gallons.

A new feature, fitted with a view to the American market, is the substitution of side and tail lamp flashing for signal arms, operated by the steering wheel control. This is rotated to right or left according to which way the car is turning, and if the switch is turned a light appears in the tail lamp on the respective side and flashes af regular intervals. Double-filament bulbs in the side lamps perform a similar flashing.

52.4 b.h.p.

Brake horse power is the same as for the Midget, 52.4 at 5,200 r.p.m. The figure for the saloon is 46 at 4,800 r.p.m. Compression ratios for the three models are identical; 7.2:1 or 7.4:1. Overall gear ratios are top 5.143, third 7.12, second 10.646 and first 18.00 to 1; comparable figures for the saloon are top 5.22, third 7.779, second 12.19 and first 18.63 to 1.

No performance figures are available but it is confidently expected that the tourer will have a top speed not far short of 80 m.p.h. The performance, too, should be even more pleasing than that of the saloon as the car is over 1cwt lighter—18¾cwt against 20cwt 22lb. No British price for this new model is available.

The general appearance, which is typically British in appearance, and which still features side lights separated from the head lights, gives an impression of a well-built and modern car, yet retaining the individuality of its make, which is somewhat rare since the war.

The photograph on the left shows the well-fitting hood, giving a wide range of visibility for the driver and passengers, and stresses the neatness of the tourer's general lines.

A large luggage boot is shown in the diagram on the right. This has been achieved without interfering with the comfort of the passengers. Note the overriders on front and rear bumpers.

GREEN-MANTLED by MICHAEL BROWN

The 1¼-litre is balanced, unobtrusive, but stylish in the traditional way. And it is still unmistakably an M.G.

THE 1¼-LITRE M.G. AFTER SIX MONTHS' ACQUAINTANCE

OBSERVANT readers (that is to say, no doubt, readers of *The Autocar*) will have noticed that the photographs in a certain series of articles frequently feature a 1¼-litre M.G., which means that the lucky author of that series is accompanied out of town by this admirable product of Abingdon. After six months of companionship I venture with caution, and with the proviso that a similar temperament on the part of the owner is necessary, to suggest that the M.G. is an ideal companion.

As a motorist I lack the virtues of some of my colleagues. Not for me the inclination (or the knowledge) to dissect my car into a super-Meccano set and then to rebuild it. But I like, when it is necessary, to be able to get at the components in need of adjustment and to carry out the work with the tools provided. Not for me, either, the technique of the trials driver or the Alpine Rally entrant; but I like to go fast when occasion demands and to take corners without more than the minimum slackening of speed. As regards styling, I am conservatively inclined, admiring function, proportion and balance, but prepared to sacrifice some of the æsthetic qualities if their presence means a reduction of function.

The picture, to the real enthusiast, may be depressing. But he may be cheered by the weakness that I have for a good central gear change, separate front seats, and revs that are not permitted to drop below a comfortable level. In other words, I am completely disinterested in the speed from which a car will pick up on top gear because I enjoy changing down, and I would not dream of letting my 1,250 c.c. pull me away from 10 m.p.h. on a ratio of 5.1 to 1. No sir; for me, 7.1 or even 10.6 to 1.

As one who was never, in the years 1939-1945, heard to mention rabbits on board ships, I had one misgiving when the M.G. became mine—it was finished in two shades of green, the body light and the wings dark (I nearly called this article Greensleeves). That was bad ju-ju; on the other hand, an ex-pilot of World War I had presented me (in 1939) with a St. Christopher which I always carry. That is good ju-ju, and the ratio of good to bad is obviously high. I forgot the two shades of green in a very short time. Right now I like them.

The M.G. is a driver's car. He settles into the seat, adjusts the steering wheel to his liking, and casts an appreciative eye at the black and white dials in the "Kimber octagons" on the polished instrument panel. He notes

that there is an ammeter, an oil pressure gauge, but no thermometer; satisfactory if not ideal. He notes that the switches are plain black knobs, and he blesses Abingdon, for the observation confirms that there is not a single distracting highlight on the facia, a fact which is also evident when the instruments are illuminated. In carping mood, he might complain that the traffic signals, operated by a knurled ring on the steering wheel boss, are returned a little too soon, but they can always be operated a second time. Of the steering wheel itself he can hardly speak too highly, for it is just right. So, too, is the steering, under all but conditions of high stress. It is light, positive, and has adequate castor action. Under real stress—when taking a corner fast—there is a slight tendency to oversteer as the i.f.s. takes its maximum load on the outside front wheel. One is not caught out by this, because such speeds are approached gradually by an intelligent driver,

Polished wood, setting off good instruments and a thin, spring-spoked steering wheel, adjustable telescopically, give the M.G. driver the slight feeling of luxury.

Clean fronts are not necessarily all-enclosed. There is little that is superfluous about this sports saloon aspect.

GREEN-MANTLED : continued

and awareness of the tendency becomes instinctive, as does counteraction. The driver who is unaware of the capabilities of i.f.s. in fast cornering would never become conscious of it.

The gear change gives me joy. I have a foolish liking for positive mechanical action. Double-pole, spring-loaded electric switches, made to carry currents of 50 amps or so, make me feel like a small boy in the cabin of the Royal Scot—if a volunteer is wanted to operate them I'm your man. Consequently the neat snick-snick of the M.G. gear lever, with not an atom of lost motion this side of the cogs, gives me the curious, sensory pleasure that belongs to such things. The cogs themselves suit my driving needs, for I have never had the feeling that such and such a ratio could do with being a bit higher or lower. A whisper of engine will move the car away from standstill, and the synchromesh is good. Just occasionally I let in the clutch and find that reverse is not properly engaged, but this is a good fault. The casual engagement of reverse is not to be recommended.

The brakes—Lockheed hydraulic—are first-class, and the hand brake (mechanical on the rear wheels) is an example of what a hand brake should be. A rigid central lever takes all the driver cares to give it, and the naked compensatory adjustment at its base gives a glimpse of cables that inspire confidence. This is still a Brake, not just a brake.

The Happy Motorist

With all this, one can understand the M.G. driver being a happy man, and that is important, for it means that, free from agitation, half-conscious misgivings, and awkwardness of manipulation, he can concentrate on the job of driving. When his attention leaves the interior as he moves off from standstill he is given additional backing. Over the bonnet is an honest side lamp, with ruby glass on top, plainly visible to mark his left side wing. The angular front, at a certain distance from the eye, drops precipitously to the road, and the positiveness of this point is, I find, of great assistance in judgment of distances. There is no such positiveness about the curving front, and the vanishing point is a matter of guesswork.

Now this ever-visible dimension is a constant for the eye of the driver, and I believe that the eye subconsciously uses it as a measuring rod for greater distances. Take it away and the eye is left in the position of the man at one side of the valley scanning the hills opposite over a sea of mist. How far off? His answer may be five miles out.

In close quarters the effect is even more beneficial. Small size overall, in conjunction with such visibility, enables the M.G. to be inserted into confined spaces with confidence. In traffic it can take gaps which other cars must shy at. When two vehicles appear abreast, coming in the opposite direction, you can assist the overtaker (even if you disapprove of his methods) by planting the left-side wheel three inches from the verge and staying there. Around the 1¼-litre a cosy enclosure of confidence is built by these attributes, and after a few thousand miles with it the driver is fearful only that some other vehicle will commit the foolish error that results in a scratched wing.

I find the 1¼-litre a happy car when it is cruising at any speed up to 60 m.p.h. Normally I do not like to see its needle above 60, but on occasion circumstances

have caused me to touch 70 m.p.h. At that speed its quite small engine becomes noticeable, and a transmission hum is evident on my particular model. None the less there is no sensation of stress, nor fear that "something might fly off." From long record and racing experience, M.G. engines have been given the ability to attain high revs, and to keep them going without protest. After prolonged spells at high speed, the 1¼ engine seems even more keyed up to the job than when it started, and, curiously enough, it frequently forgets to run on after such a burst, although it may do so after a quarter-mile from the filling station at 20 m.p.h. The phenomenon is easily stopped by opening the throttle wide immediately after switching off. One thing that puzzles me is the quick drop of water in the header tank. I believe it is spillage, and having gone down to finger-tip the level will go no farther ; but as I like unscrewing the heavy plated cap and balancing it in my hand (I reckon nothing of the h.p. which goes on such vanity) I have not let matters go far enough to be sure.

If I am to utilize figures for an argument I have to force myself to extract the slide rule from its case. Consequently I haven't a clue as to averages on the M.G. Believe it or not, I do not know the exact mileage from my home to the offices of this journal. All I can say is that I have several times driven myself into a corner with regard to time, but that the 1¼-litre has invariably got me out of it. Petrol consumption is in the region of 30 m.p.g. and oil consumption virtually nil (10,000 miles). Likewise it has reliably started, with minimum use of the choke ; indeed, it is easily possible to over-choke. At night, the lights live well up to the speed, and in the half-light I bless the ruby glasses to the side lamps. When they are on the whole world, *and* the driver, know it.

I would not change a thing on the car, although some would like a larger luggage locker. Hobo-minded, I tend to travel—as does my regular passenger—with a toothbrush and pyjamas, so we do not mind the comparatively small space ; in any case, the back seat is normally unoccupied. Being human, I am a snob at heart. Small boys do not say, "Coo, etc., etc.," but the more knowing ones have been known to point out to their fellows that *that* is an M.G., and the wealth of emphasis behind the initials shows that they are *au fait* on their Goldie Gardner. I was immensely flattered the other morning when a near neighbour, an R.A.F. three-ringer with a plentiful plastering of fruit salad, made a complete circuit of the car as it stood outside my gate, one eyebrow cocked appreciatively. *Very* flattering.

"The angular front, at a certain distance from the eye, drops precipitously to the road," a help in judging distances, says the author.

The Motor Road Test No. 11/51——

Make : M.G.   **Type :** 1¼-litre Saloon
Makers : M.G. Car Co. Ltd., Abingdon-on-Thames, Berks.

Dimensions and Seating

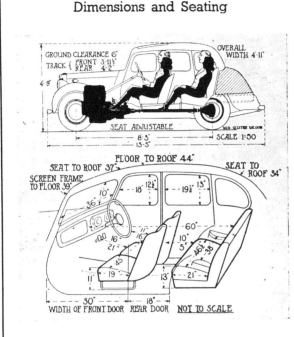

In Brief

Price £565 plus purchase tax £315 7s. 9d. equals £880 7s. 9d.
Capacity .. .. .. 1,250 c.c.
Unladen kerb weight.. 20½ cwt.
Fuel consumption .. 29.5 m.p.g.
Maximum speed .. 69.6 m.p.h.
Maximum speed on 1 in 20 gradient .. 56 m.p.h.
Maximum top gear gradient .. .. 1 in 12.5
Acceleration
10-30 m.p.h. in top.. 12 secs.
0.50 m.p.h. through gears.. .. 18.8 secs.
Gearing, 14.6 m.p.h. in top at 1,000 r.p.m., 61.8 m.p.h. at 2,500 ft. per min. piston speed.

Specification

Engine
Cylinders 4
Bore .. .. .. 66.5 mm.
Stroke .. .. .. 90 mm.
Cubic capacity .. .. 1,250 c.c.
Piston area .. .. 21.6 sq. in.
Valves .. .. Pushrod, o.h.v.
Compression ratio .. 7.2/7.4 : 1
Max. power .. .. 46 b.h.p.
   at .. .. .. 4,800 r.p.m.
Piston speed at max. b.h.p. 2,835 ft. per min.
Carburetter Single S.U. 1¼ in. semi-downdraught
Ignition .. .. .. Coil
Sparking plugs .. Champion L.10S
Fuel pump .. .. S.U. electric
Oil filter .. .. Own, full-flow
Transmission
Clutch 7¼ in. Borg and Beck single dry plate
Top gear (s/m) 5.143
3rd gear (s/m) 7.121
2nd gear (s/m) 10.646
1st gear 18.00
Propeller shaft Hardy Spicer, needle bearing
Final drive .. .. Spiral bevel
Chassis
Brakes Lockheed hydraulic, handbrake cable to rear only
Brake drum diameter .. .. 9 in.
Friction lining area .. 104 sq. in.
Suspension : Front, independent (coil spring) Rear, semi-elliptic
Shock absorbers :
  Front } Luvax-Girling piston type
  Rear
Tyres .. .. 5.25 × 16 e.l.p.
Steering
Steering gear .. .. Rack and pinion
Turning circle .. .. 35 ft.
Turns of steering wheel, lock to lock .. 2⅓
Performance factors (at laden weight as tested)
Piston area, sq. in. per ton .. 18.0
Brake lining area, sq. in. per ton .. 86
Specific displacement, litres per ton mile 2,140
(Fully described in " The Motor," May 14, 1947

Test Conditions

Strong crosswind, heavy showers, dry road for acceleration and braking tests. Pool petrol.

Test Data

ACCELERATION TIMES on Two Upper Ratios

	Top	3rd.
10-30 m.p.h.	2.0 secs.	9.0 secs.
20-40 m.p.h.	14.0 secs.	9.7 secs.
30-50 m.p.h.	18.0 secs.	13.8 secs.
40-60 m.p.h.	22.6 secs.	—

ACCELERATION TIMES Through Gears

0-30 m.p.h.	6.1 secs.
0-40 m.p.h.	10.8 secs.
0-50 m.p.h.	18.8 secs.
0-60 m.p.h.	29.9 secs.
Standing Quarter Mile	23.8 secs.

MAXIMUM SPEEDS

Flying Quarter Mile
Mean for four opposite runs .. 69.6 m.p.h.
Best time equals .. .. 75 m.p.h.

Speed in Gears
Max. speed in 3rd gear .. .. 55 m.p.h.
Max. speed in 2nd gear .. .. 37 m.p.h.
Max. speed in 1st gear .. .. 25 m.p.h.

WEIGHT

Unladen kerb weight .. 20½ cwt.
Front/rear weight distribution 48/52
Weight laden as tested .. 24 cwt.

FUEL CONSUMPTION

47 m.p.g. at constant 30 m.p.h.
40 m.p.g. at constant 40 m.p.h.
33 m.p.g. at constant 50 m.p.h.
27.5 m.p.g. at constant 60 m.p.h.
Overall consumption for 288 miles,
9.75 gallons, equals 29.5 m.p.g.

INSTRUMENTS

Speedometer at 30 m.p.h. .. 8% fast
Speedometer at 60 m.p.h. .. 13% fast
Distance recorder .. .. 2% fast

HILL CLIMBING (At steady speeds)

Max. top gear speed on 1 in 20 .. .. 56 m.p.h.
Max. top gear speed on 1 in 15 .. .. 48 m.p.h.
Max. gradient on top gear .. 1 in 12.5 (Tapley 180 lb./ton)
Max. gradient on 3rd gear .. 1 in 9.3 (Tapley 240 lb./ton)
Max. gradient on 2nd gear .. 1 in 7 (Tapley 320 lb./ton)

BRAKES at 30 m.p.h.

0.98g. retardation (=30.6 ft. stopping distance)

Maintenance

Fuel tank : 8 gallons. **Sump :** 9 pints, S.A.E. 30. **Gearbox :** 1½ pints, S.A.E. 140. **Rear axle :** 1½ pints, S.A.E. 140. **Steering gear :** Rack and pinion. **Radiator :** 13½ pints (drain taps). **Chassis lubrication :** By grease gun to 13 points. **Ignition timing :** T.D.C. **Spark plug gap :** 0.020 in. to 0.022 in. **Contact breaker gap :** 0.010 in. to 0.012 in. **Valve timing :** Inlet opens 11° b.t.d.c., inlet shuts 57° a.b.d.c. Exhaust opens 52° b.b.d.c., exhaust shuts 24° a.t.d.c. **Tappet clearances (hot) :** inlet, 0.019 in., exhaust, 0.019 in. **Front wheel toe-in :** Nil. **Camber angle :** Nil to –1½° on bump. **Castor angle :** 1° ± ¼°. **Tyre pressures :** Front, 23 lb., rear, 25 lb. **Brake fluid :** Lockheed. **Battery :** Lucas STXW9A. 51AH at 10 hr. rate. **Lamp bulbs :** All Lucas. O/s head, No. 54, 36 watt, 12 volt; N/s head, No. 171, 36/36 watt, 12 volt. Side : No. 207, 6 watt, 12 volt. Reverse : No. 1, 24 watt, 12 volt. Panel : 986/987, 2.2 watt, 12 volt. Ignition : 970, 0.5 watt, 2.5 volt. Trafficator : 256, 3 watt, 12 volt. Fog : 87, 60 watt, 12 volt. Interior : 207, 6 watt, 12 volt.   Ref.

—The M.G. Y-type 1¼ litre Saloon

An Economical Four-seater Saloon with Notable Ease of Maintenance

Just as this gear lever calls to mind the now-forgotten cliche "falls readily to hand," so does the forward view through the somewhat narrow screen bring the recollection of another lost phrase, to wit, "both front wings are visible." In the case of the M.G., they are clearly marked by the separate side lamps, and this undoubtedly assists in gauging the width of the car and helping the driver through heavy traffic and confined spaces.

Finally, although the body is made from

SENSIBLE SCHEME—The luggage-carrying capacity of the M.G. can be enlarged by using the locker door as a tray, beneath which the spare wheel and tools are accessibly housed. Inbuilt hydraulic jacks are provided.

THE current M.G. 1¼ saloon was introduced to the British market in mid-May 1947 and, in the subsequent four years, only the most minor modifications have been introduced. The car is therefore one of the very first post-war models, and it is an open secret that, in conception, it dates back to the immediate pre-war period at the Abingdon factory. It is therefore not surprising that, in contrast with later designs with all-enveloping form, the M.G. has a distinctly old-fashioned appearance, whilst a study of the specification reveals that a number of features now accepted as common fitments, such as the so-called air-conditioning system, self-parking windscreen wipers, steering-column gear lever, and bench-type front seat, are absent. But there are many who will rejoice that the appearance continues a long tradition and others who will shed few tears over the absence of some of the features set out above.

Early Virtues Retained

This apart, after only a few miles at the wheel of the car, one becomes very deeply impressed by the retention of many old-fashioned virtues which have in large measure been washed into the sea of time by the inexorable flow of progress.

Putting first things first, both driver and front passenger find themselves in individually adjustable seats, well formed to give sideways support, and with an accessible and reasonably efficient hand brake placed between them. The extensible steering column makes it possible to place the wheel in the best position for the driver, and the instruments immediately in front of him are of sensible size with sober inscriptions. They are mounted in a facia panel made of what an American salesman proudly called "genuine tree wood," and the whole of the left side of the panel is given up to a really large locker which will comfortably hold a small handbag in addition to other miscellaneous articles.

The necessary switch gear is disposed around the right hand side of the panel,

and in the centre is a now almost-forgotten handle which will open the front windscreen and will thus prove of invaluable assistance when fog be met upon the road. A further rare feature, but one perhaps even more appreciated by many motorists, is the sliding roof, whilst immediately ahead of the hand brake a short gear lever connects to a four-speed box giving a combination which is superlative in itself, and almost comically superior to the average steering-column type.

steel pressings, the interior furnishings, which include a number of wooden fillets, act as most effective sound dampers, and, although the engine in itself is far from quiet, one hears the noise by itself and not, as so often today, as "the echo of a cry." This freedom from reverberation is matched by a seemingly complete absence of draughts.

The points which have been mentioned will perhaps make it clear that we thoroughly enjoyed driving the M.G. 1¼-litre

OPENING UP—The car is one of the few saloons available today offering a combination of sliding roof and opening windscreen. This picture also shows the separate seats and good position of the central gear lever

EASY ACCESS — The traditional bonnet style gives full accessibility for components such as carburetter, petrol pump, wiper motor, and fuse box.

saloon and thought it an admirable vehicle for everyday purposes.

A glance at the test data shows that it is not outstanding either in maximum speed or acceleration, although all the figures were probably rather worse than normal owing to exceptionally bad weather experienced during the test period. Nevertheless, a genuine maximum speed of practically 70 m.p.h., representing a shade over 80 m.p.h. on the speedometer supplied to us, is certainly adequate for most normal motoring, whilst gradients steeper than 1 in 10 can be tackled at quite high speed if the really excellent gear-change is used for the engagement of third speed. In traffic, second gear is particularly effective, and the performance on this ratio is aided by the ability of the engine to soar up to 5,000 r.p.m. with no hesitation.

Real Economy

Again postulating free use of the gear box, really high average speeds can be accomplished and, even when driven very hard, the fuel consumption falls below 30 m.p.g. by a decimal point only, so that well over 30 m.p.g. could obviously be obtained if economy of running were thought to be more important than time spent on the journey.

With petrol at present prices, both here and in the world at large, this in itself is an important recommendation, but the merits of the M.G. are certainly not exhausted by a consideration of the utilitarian aspects of speed, acceleration and fuel economy. It is, above all, an exceedingly pleasing car to drive and in which to be driven. Not only does one welcome the sound-deadening properties of the body, but one also rejoices in the relatively low level of wind noise, these two features together making it quite easy to listen to radio programmes at sustained speeds of 60 m.p.h. The suspension may be thought a little on the hard side by 1951 standards, but there is an agreeable freedom from pitch and only moderate roll.

Driving the car on fast corners demands a certain degree of practice, for the car has over-steering characteristics which verge, perhaps, on the exaggerated. As a consequence, an almost imperceptible nudge on the steering wheel will set in motion a train of dynamic and geometric sequences which will virtually steer the car round a corner of quite modest radius, whilst, on the other hand, substantial movement of the wheel, particularly when

cornering at speed, may be followed by the dreaded side slip, because the tail of the car comes round quite quickly if the permissible limits of adhesion are exceeded. Owing, however, to the high gearing and positive connection in the rack-and-pinion steering gear, correction of the skid presents no difficulties to an alert driver nor, within the maximum speed limits of this particular car, does the over-steering quality generate any problems in control on straight roads, although there is naturally a certain sensitivity to high cross winds.

Once the driver is used to the characteristics of the car, cornering becomes an extraordinarily easy and effortless activity and the car shows a power of manœuvrability completely consonant with the well-known slogan of the makers.

Reverting now to some more practical points in connection with this car, one has to recognise that it is a four-seater, as although three persons can be carried on the back seat, the width is such that this number could only be tolerated for very short distances. With the designed maximum load, however, everyone is seated in above-average comfort and there is an armrest separating the two rear seat pas-

sengers. Their outlook benefits considerably from the six-light body and each passenger has an individual ashtray. The rear window can be masked by a blind, the rooflight is of adequate brightness for book or map reading in either front or rear seats, and the headlights give a forward view well up to the speed of the car.

Luggage Platform

The space enclosed by the luggage locker is on the small side by modern standards, but, against this, the locker lid is hinged at its base and can be swung out to form a platform by which means really large pieces of luggage can be accommodated. The spare wheel and tools are carried separately, immediately above the fuel tank, and the accident of a nail penetrating a front tyre brought home the very real worth of the hydraulic "Jackall" system as a saver of both time and temper. Owing to the fuel economy, the car has a range of over 200 miles, despite the somewhat meagre tank capacity of 8 gallons, but on a car of this type, this obviously is a feature which could well be improved.

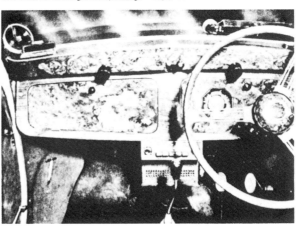

FINE FINISH—The well-finished woodwork in the body interior, the neat lay-out of the instruments and the exceptionally large dashboard locker are clearly shown in this illustration. The radio set fitted is available as an optional extra.

The type of front suspension and steering linkage used involves easier and less-frequent attention to lubrication than normal, whilst any attention required by the engine is, of course, very greatly assisted by the use of the old-fashioned type of front end and bonnet.

Summing up, therefore, we found this car to be notably attractive in respect of owner and passenger convenience, economy, and ease of maintenance. Once the peculiarity of the handling has been mastered (not a difficult process) the car is exceedingly pleasant to drive and it has an all-round performance which is more than adequate for the needs of the overwhelming majority of motorists.

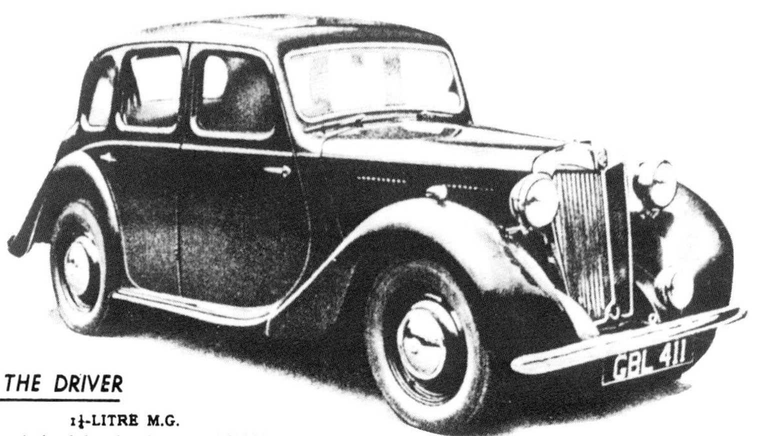

The external appearance of the "1¼" is traditional in every respect; separate wings, running boards and external radiator filler cap and head lamps are all retained. A bright interior is provided by the six-light arrangement of the windows.

DATA FOR THE DRIVER

1¼-LITRE M.G.

PRICE, with saloon body, £565, plus £315 7s 9d British purchase tax. Total (in Great Britain), £880 7s 9d.

ENGINE: 10.97 h.p. (R.A.C. rating), 4 cylinders, overhead valves, 66.5×90 mm, 1,250 c.c. Brake Horse-power: 45 at 4,800 r.p.m. Compression Ratio: 7.2 to 1. Max. Torque: 63.75 lb ft at 2,600 r.p.m. 14.6 m.p.h. per 1,000 r.p.m. on top gear.

WEIGHT: 20 cwt 0 qr 0 lb (2,240 lb). Front wheels 48.5 per cent; rear wheels 51.5 per cent. LB per C.C.: 1.78. B.H.P. per TON: 45.0.

TYRE SIZE: 5.25—16in on bolt-on steel disc wheels.

TANK CAPACITY: 8 English gallons. Approximate fuel consumption range, 27-34 m.p.g. (10.5—8.3 litres per 100 km).

TURNING CIRCLE: 35ft (L and R). Steering wheel movement from lock to lock: 2¾ turns. LIGHTING SET: 12-volt.

MAIN DIMENSIONS: Wheelbase, 8ft 3in. Track, 3ft 11⅜in (front); 4ft 2in (rear). Overall length, 13ft 5$\frac{1}{16}$in; width, 4ft 10¼in; height, 4ft 9in. Minimum Ground Clearance: 6in.

ACCELERATION

Overall gear ratios	*From steady m.p.h. of* 10-30 sec	20-40 sec	30-50 sec	40-60 sec
5.143 to 1	13.9	14.0	15.2	19.0
7.121 to 1	11.1	9.9	11.6	—
10.646 to 1	7.0	7.9	—	—
18.000 to 1	—	—	—	—

From rest through gears to:—

	sec		sec
30 m.p.h. . .	6.7	60 m.p.h. . .	29.3
50 m.p.h. . .	18.2		

SPEEDS ON GEARS:

(*by Electric speedometer*)	M.p.h. (normal and max)	K.p.h. (normal and max)
1st	18—24	29—39
2nd	34—41	55—66
3rd	50—62	80—100
Top	70	113

Speedometer correction by Electric Speedometer:—

Car Speedometer		Electric Speedometer m.p.h.
10	=	10.0
20	=	19.0
30	=	28.0
40	=	36.5
50	=	44.5
60	=	54.0
70	=	62.0
80	=	70.0

WEATHER: Dry, warm; wind negligible.

Acceleration figures are the means of several runs in opposite directions.

Described in "The Autocar" of September 9, 1949.

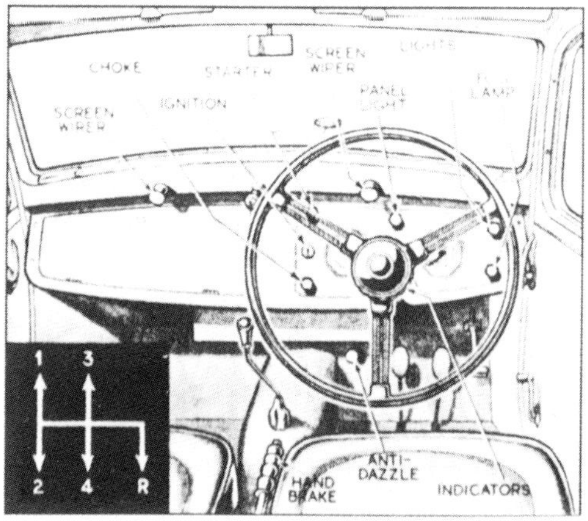

1¼-LITRE M.G. SALOON

WHEN a model continues in production without basic alterations for well over four years, as applies to the 1¼-litre M.G., and remains a successful and appreciated car, it must obviously possess decided points of merit. So noteworthy is this state of affairs in this instance that, the original Road Test of the model having appeared as long ago as in *The Autocar* dated May 9, 1947, it seemed worth while investigating the road behaviour of the current edition, almost entirely unaltered though it is. The situation is the more interesting in view of the fact that, fundamentally, this car is a survival—that is, in its perpetuation of the traditional style of appearance and general arrangement in a car of relatively small engine size and overall dimensions.

Surely, one reflects, it must be because it is a survival, and in some degree unique today, that the model has continued to be successful in a specialized market. Virtually alone is it now in offering the form of external appearance to which many keener motorists still cling, in spite of the wider acceptance of shapes that have come to be called modern; but more than that, it represents the style of car which can still be regarded as typically British, that is, before fashion dictated slab sides, faired-in lamps and radiators disguised to vanishing point.

A clear-cut assessment can be laid down of the 1¼ M.G. It is strictly a four-seater saloon. It was not originally intended to be a really high-performance model, but rather a family car of good quality, with sporting characteristics and good handling qualities. It has an overhead valve engine of a size which restricts its thirst for fuel to a degree that is comforting in these days of high costs, yet provides a performance which has its surprises.

Rather specially is it possible to comment in almost affectionate terms on this model, for, quite apart from this present test, unusual staff experience has been obtained of this version of M.G. An example which has been in *The Autocar's* service for the past four years has endeared itself to its principal users, has proved a most reliable car, and, incidentally, at the end of its fourth year has recently completed a not unarduous Continental tour of some 2,000 miles, fully laden, with very satisfactory results. Therefore it is possible to offer unusual expressions of comment, quite apart from the general run of expressions more properly belonging to these reviews.

It has been remarked that the performance contains surprises. At first experience of the latest car, in town traffic,

The well-known M.G. radiator grille is predominant in this view, while in spite of the use of i.f.s. the valances below the bonnet sides might be supposed to cover dumb-irons, which, of course, do not exist.

A clever matching of curves results in a pleasing rear view; the sweep of the rear wings extends back to the rear of the car. The rearward opening front doors and forward opening rear doors are pivoted on common external hinges.

one is reminded of its handiness, its ability, because of its compact size, to make the best use of traffic openings, its convenience for parking in congested conditions, and its useful liveliness of acceleration with only moderate use of the gear box, coupled with a quite satisfactory flexibility on top gear. Take it next on a main-road journey under conditions of comparative freedom from other traffic, and let there be necessity for hurrying, as applied in this instance, and there will be renewed for the former enthusiast for the model a real regard for the average speed abilities it can pull out of its relatively small engine.

Even with allowance made for a decidedly optimistic speedometer in the upper range, the cruising speed, without overstress being suggested, is a genuine 55-60 m.p.h., and it can go up to a genuine 70 and still feel within its margins. It is possible to put well over 40 miles into an hour even on the never really helpful English road, with its speed limit restrictions in built-up areas and manifold hazards. The M.G. hums along at speeds up to its limit. There is a little fine vibration noticeable, more so on this particular car than has been experienced on others of this type.

The handling and the controls are very much a part of the quality layout and character. The rack and pinion steering is of high merit, being light yet accurate and safe feeling, and transmitting to the steering wheel no more than an occasional twitch from the road wheels over such a surface as stone setts; it has a slight over-steering tendency. It is the kind of steering that calls for no more than the driver to rest his hands on the wheel and bear rather than

haul on it for cornering. It is quite high-geared steering, yet remains light and has useful castor action.

Alone among the cars made by the Nuffield Organization (the M.G. is still produced at Abingdon-on-Thames), the M.G. has coil springs in its independent front suspension. One receives the impression that the suspension is firmer than on the earliest models. It behaves very well laterally for cornering and gives a stability which makes the car feel safe during fast driving. There is a certain amount of vertical motion of limited amplitude over surfaces that are less than good, but the net effect is of a car that rides very well in the rear as well as the front seats.

No hard words can be levelled against the braking system; in fact the reverse, for these Lockheed hydraulics do their job extremely well without needing heavy pedal pressure, and have the high asset that on the great proportion of braking occasions there is an ample margin.

The driving position is well contrived, with a neat, thin-rimmed spring wheel at a most satisfactory angle, and telescopically adjustable on its column when a locking lever is freed, the operation not calling for the application of a spanner. The pedals, though of comparatively small size, are fairly well spaced, and the gear change is one of the delights of the kind of driver to whom the M.G. is likely to appeal. The lever rises centrally from a tunnel over the gear box, and in length is between the full-scale old-type central lever and the short remote control pattern that is now equally rare. Its action retains the rigidity of the

The deep rear seat has a pull-down centre arm rest, ash trays are fitted in the backs of the front seats and pull straps are provided to the front of the rear quarter light.

There is an air of quality about the M.G. interior. Pockets in the doors, an opening windscreen, an immediately adjustable steering wheel and an ideally placed hand brake lever all add to personal comfort. (Inset) The polished walnut veneer facia panel and glove locker lid, together with the octagonal instrument groupings, are typical of British quality practice. A time delay traffic signals switch is fitted on the steering wheel. Radio is an extra.

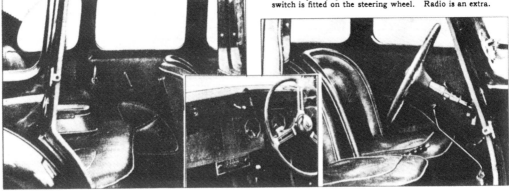

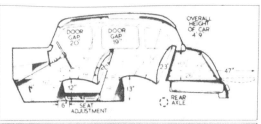

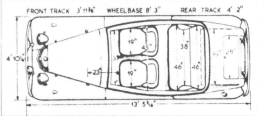

Measurements in these scale body diagrams are taken with
the driving seat in the central position of fore and aft adjustment and with the seat cushions uncompressed.

Because the locker lid is hinged at the bottom the useful
luggage carrying capacity can be considerably increased
by using the lid as a platform. (Inset) A separate lower
compartment houses the spare wheels and tools.

latter style of much appreciated gear lever, and the synchromesh and selector action is such that the lever moves with a
definite snick into second, third and top. Changing can be
quite quick, if required, without entirely beating the synchromesh. The indirect gear ratios are distinctly useful;
third is most useful at times for a brisk acceleration or a
quick climb, 50 m.p.h. being comfortable on this gear, whilst
second copes with gradients in the 1 in 6 (16 per cent) category.

A tall driver, especially, notices a rather shallow windscreen which, incidentally, can be opened by means of a

central winding control, again a feature which is a survival
The driver has a view of the right-hand wing in a right-
hand drive car and of the left-hand wing lamp. In front
of him is a neat grouping of instruments—which include
an ammeter and an oil pressure gauge, but not a water
thermometer—and of the minor controls, which are all of
push-and-pull type. These are set in a most attractively
finished veneered facia, a finish which is applied also to the
door cappings, and which in conjunction with the good
leather upholstery, available in colours contrasting with the
exterior finish, provides an essentially British quality car
interior.

The front seats are separate and individually adjustable—another feature that is "old style" to good effect in
many people's view. The hand brake lever is set most
conveniently between the front seats. It requires to be
pulled hard on to hold the car on an appreciable gradient.
In the side of the facia opposite to the instruments is a
large cupboard with lid, although this is not lockable. A
really useful view is provided by the driving mirror.

An excellent feature in many people's opinion, again, is
the provision of a sliding roof even though it is of small
area, as well as of another item of equipment which is
passing, a rear window blind. The traffic signals are controlled by a knurled ring at the centre of the steering wheel,
operating a time switch that automatically returns the
signals irrespective of the position of the steering wheel.
One would prefer to have the forward window winders
mounted higher on the doors and thus more readily accessible without reaching down and forward. The rear seat
has a well-arranged central arm rest as well as elbow rests,
and good support in upright rather than reclining positions
is given by all the seats.

From previous extended experience of the model it can
be said that the head lamps give a good beam, and included
in the standard equipment is a separately switched fog
lamp. Another practical item of the standard specification
is a Smiths Jackall four-wheel hydraulic jacking system.
Engine starting from cold is immediate and little use of the
mixture control is needed before the engine settles down
without hesitation, although it is sensitive to air temperature in this respect. It displays pinking when accelerating
from the lower speeds on the low-octane British Pool petrol,
as well as some running-on after being switched off, but, as
is general experience with fairly high compression units, is
a revelation in these respects when better quality fuel is
available.

The experienced motorist in particular has only to look
at the car externally to label it as a thoroughbred. Specialized items of equipment have been referred to already, and
the car is undoubtedly well turned out in this respect, as
also in actual finish. It has its definite appeal to the seasoned motorist who appreciates the better things in cars, and
also it is remarkably easy to handle and not in the slightest
degree tricky for the type who may be called the more
ordinary motorist.

A single S.U. carburettor is supplied with air via the cleaner
mounted over the rocker cover. A small breather pipe is
provided with filtration by fitting it into the lower side of
the air cleaner. The scuttle mounted hydraulic jacking
control system can be seen in front of the ignition coil.

The M.G. saloon is one of the few small cars that retains a traditional four-door six-light body style. It also is fitted with a sunshine roof. Features such as separate head lamps and running boards are still retained.

1¼-LITRE M.G. SALOON

FOR many years the two letters M.G. have been dear to the hearts of a large number of enthusiasts. Through the years the company has produced a wide variety of models, ranging from a multiplicity of Midgets (Magic or otherwise) to saloons of up to 2.6 litres. At the moment production is concentrated on two models, the open two-seater known as the TD Midget and a four-seater saloon mechanically similar to the open car, known in its latest version as the YB. The saloon is one of the very few examples available in this country of a modern 1,250 c.c. engine and chassis fitted with traditional quality coachwork. It is of a size and performance that would suit the requirements of large numbers of motorists, yet it is compact and economical and very handy in congested areas, and can be housed in a quite small garage.

Few modifications have been made to this model since it was introduced about five years ago. However, two detail changes to the chassis have recently been made. A hypoid rear axle unit has replaced its spiral bevel counterpart, and an anti-roll bar is now fitted to the front suspension. It might be thought that an engine of only 1,250 c.c. in a fully equipped saloon body would produce only a very ordinary performance. But this is not the case. In part, perhaps, because of its sporting background, coupled with plenty of common sense on the part of its designers, the car does not protest at being driven hard. On the other hand, it is not in any way rough. In fact, it has in addition a number of qualities desirable in a small, smart town carriage.

On the open road some 40 miles can be put into an hour without working the willing horses unduly, while under favourable conditions a decidedly better average is possible if the driver is really trying. Although it is a quite flexible

DATA

PRICE (basic), with saloon body, £635.
British purchase tax, £354 5s 6d.
Total (in Great Britain), £989 5s 6d.
Extras : Radio £24 15s 2d.
　　　　Heater £10 17s 10d.

ENGINE : Capacity 1,250 c.c. (76.28 cu. in.).
Number of cylinders : 4.
Bore and stroke : 66.5 × 90 mm. (2.62 × 3.54in).
Valve gear : o.h.v., push rods and rockers.
Compression ratio : 7.2 to 1.
B.H.P. : 46 at 4,800 r.p.m. (37.5 B.H.P. per ton laden).
Torque : 58.5 lb ft at 2,400 r.p.m.
M.P.H. per 1,000 r.p.m. on top gear, 14.42.

WEIGHT (with 5 galls fuel), 21 cwt (2,341 lb).
Weight distribution (per cent) : 49 F ; 51 R.
Laden as tested : 24½ cwt (2,755 lb).
Lb per c.c. (laden) 2.2.

TYRES : 5.50—15in.
Pressures (lb per sq in) : 23 F ; 25 R.

TANK CAPACITY : 8 Imperial gallons.
Oil sump, 9 pints.
Cooling system, 13¼ pints.

TURNING CIRCLE : 33ft 6in (L and R).
Steering wheel turns (lock to lock) : 2½.

DIMENSIONS : Wheelbase 8ft 3in.
Track : 3ft 11½in (F) ; 4ft 2in (R).
Length (overall) : 13ft 8in.
Height : 4ft 9in.
Width : 4ft 11in.
Ground clearance : 5½in.
Frontal area : 18.7 sq ft (approx).

ELECTRICAL SYSTEM : 12-volt 52 ampère-hour battery.
Head lights : Double dip, 42–36 watt.

SUSPENSION : Front, independent with wishbones and coil springs.
Rear, half-elliptic springs.

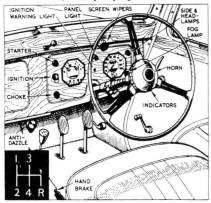

PERFORMANCE

1¼-LITRE M.G. SALOON

ACCELERATION : from constant speeds.
Speed, Gear Ratios and time in sec.

M.P.H.	5.125 to 1	7.098 to 1	10.609 to 1	17.938 to 1
10—30	15.4	10.5	7.1	—
20—40	15.3	10.4	8.4	—
30—50	16.0	11.8	—	—
40—60	22.0	—	—	—

From rest through gears to :

M.P.H.	sec.
30	6.9
50	18.4
60	30.4

Standing quarter mile, 24.5 sec.

SPEED ON GEARS :

Gear		M.P.H. (normal and max.)	K.P.H. (normal and max.)
Top	(mean)	71	114
	(best)	75	121
3rd		54—59	87—95
2nd		30—40	48—64
1st		14—22	23—35

TRACTIVE RESISTANCE : 18 lb per ton at 10 M.P.H.

TRACTIVE EFFORT :

	Pull (lb per ton)	Equivalent Gradient
Top	154	1 in 15
Third	233	1 in 8.8
Second	320	1 in 6.5

BRAKES

Efficiency	Pedal Pressure (lb)
85 per cent	146
84 per cent	100
49 per cent	50

FUEL CONSUMPTION :
26.5 m.p.g. overall for 265 miles (10.66 litres per 100 km).
Approximate normal range 24—28 m.p.g. (11.8—10.1 litres per 100 km).
Fuel : British Pool.

WEATHER : Dry surface, wind fresh.
Air temperature 52 degrees F.
Acceleration figures are the means of several runs in opposite directions.
Tractive effort and resistance obtained by Tapley meter.
Model described in The Autocar of September 9, 1949, and January 4, 1952.

SPEEDOMETER CORRECTION : M.P.H.

Car speedometer	10	20	30	40	50	60	70	80	85
True speed	10	19	28	37	46	56	63	70	75

engine, it does not like to be allowed to slog, and to get the best out of it the gears should be freely used. Top gear will cope with normal main road gradients, yet third is often kinder if the car is well laden. On second gear it will climb most steeper hills, including a 1 in 5 test gradient.

Unlike the other cars produced by the Nuffield Organization, which use torsion bars for the front suspension, the M.G. employs coil springs at the front, in conjunction with half-elliptic springs for the rear suspension. This arrangement results in a very stable car and the firm, controlled ride inspires confidence. There is no marked pitching, nor is the suspension sufficiently hard to cause the ride to be rough or jerky when traversing bad surfaces. Cornering in the M.G. is particularly pleasant and the effect of the anti-roll bar is distinctly beneficial, there being very little roll on corners; also this addition appears to have eliminated the slight oversteer tendency mentioned when the car was last tested. Under normal conditions, with two up, the car now has a slight tendency to understeer, although in the fully laden condition a slight amount of oversteer was experienced. As it happened, the car was handled on snow-

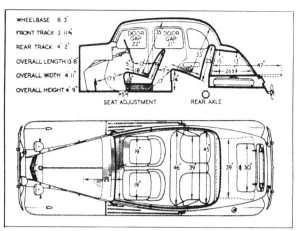

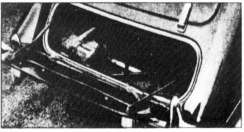

Measurements in these $\frac{1}{8}$in to 1ft scale body diagrams are taken with the driving seat in the central position of fore and aft adjustment and with the rear cushions uncompressed.

The luggage locker has a platform type of lid which provides a useful addition to the carrying capacity. A separate lower compartment with detachable lid houses the spare wheel and tools.

Both front seats are adjustable for leg length by means of catches placed half way along the outer seat runners. Pockets are provided on the front doors, and the window winders are placed low down and to the front.

covered roads for an appreciable distance during the test. Under these conditions it inspired exceptional confidence and by its precise response made them almost enjoyable.

The rack and pinion steering, with 2¼ turns from lock to lock, is very positive, with no lost motion or any suspicion of "rubber rods" in the mechanism. It has a nice feel and a good self-centring action; it is reasonably light, yet quick and very responsive steering. A slight amount of road shock is transmitted back through the wheel at times, but this is not in any way excessive.

The gear change mechanism has a lever which can best be described as midway between the earlier conventional central lever and a remote control mechanism of the kind fitted to the M.G. Midget open two-seater. It is very rigid and positive in operation. The synchromesh has a nice feel and is sufficiently effective to prevent the mechanism being crashed or beaten unless particularly snappy changes are made. The clutch has a light and smooth action and is pleasant to operate.

Hydraulically operated brakes working on the two-leading-shoe principle at the front are well up to their job. Pedal pressure required for maximum efficiency is fairly high, yet for normal road conditions very good results are obtained without pressing particularly hard. At all times the car stops in no uncertain manner and the brakes maintain perfect balance. Under the severe conditions imposed during performance testing no brake fade or judder was experienced, nor was there any noticeable increase in free pedal travel subsequently. The hand brake lever, located between the separate front seats, is in a very convenient position and one which enables a good leverage to be applied to it when necessary.

A folding central arm rest is fitted in the rear seat, and holding straps are attached to the rear pillars. The rear window winders are placed above the door pockets. There is a narrow shelf at the top of the rear seat backs.

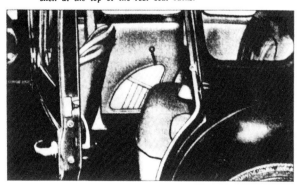

From the front the familiar rectangular grille gives the car a neat, traditional appearance. The filler cap is genuine. Deep over-riders add a modern touch, and give useful protection.

A waist line starting at the bonnet runs to the back of the body, where it blends into the sweeping rear wing. The quick-action fuel filler cap protrudes through the left rear wing. A roller blind, driver-operated, serves the rear window.

Driving position in the 1¼-litre is very good. From the driving seat both front wings are clearly visible. The windscreen pillars are of average thickness, but the absence of a pivoted quarter light in the side windows improves three-quarter front visibility. The driving mirror, too, is well placed, and provides a clear view of what is going on behind. It would perhaps be better for some sizes of driver on long journeys if the curved backs of the front seats were higher to give more support to the shoulders, and also if the seat cushions were made a little longer to give more support to the leg muscles. Both front seats are adjustable for leg length, and the seat springing is comfortable and firm.

A thin-rimmed spring-spoked steering wheel mounted on a column which is particularly easily adjustable for length —and firmly locked in the required position—enables a useful variation of position to be made, and also the wheel is set at a comfortable angle. The clutch and brake pedals are quite small, but they are well positioned and comfortable to operate. There is also room between the tunnel over the gear box and the clutch pedal for the driver's left leg. This is not only advantageous in any case, but also is actually necessary with this car, because of the position of the dip switch, which is mounted fairly well forward on the toe board. The throttle pedal, too, is pleasant to operate and nicely positioned.

All the minor controls are mounted directly in front of the driver on the facia panel. They are well spaced, so that there is no confusion when operating knobs of a similar size and shape in the dark. These include the switch for a fog lamp fitted as standard equipment.

A longitudinally hinged bonnet is still used on the M.G. A single S.U. carburettor on this model is fitted with a light alloy intake duct coupled to the transverse air cleaner. In spite of appearances, it is possible to oil the carburettor piston damper without removing the air cleaner. The battery is completely enclosed in the case to which the electric petrol pump is attached. The windscreen wiper motor is mounted on the bulkhead Owners of older models will note the additional hoses for the heater system.

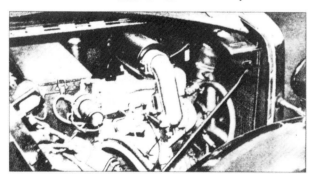

Perhaps one of the things that is most impressive about the 1¼-litre is that it is designed to carry only four people. The consequent compactness gives it a much more solid feel, and also allows it to be made more silent, than would be possible without a prohibitive increase in weight if a larger body were used.

Features seldom found on post-war cars are a sliding roof, an opening windscreen and a rear window blind. The M.G. has all three. The interior of this six-light saloon is very nicely finished. The facia in particular deserves mention, as it is tastefully styled in polished wood. The left side is completely occupied by a large locker with a flush-fitting lid. Polished wood cappings are used on all the doors, which are trimmed to match the seats, while the floor is covered with very dark carpet. A full complement of ashtrays is fitted. The screenwiper blades are of a good length and well positioned, yet they could, with advantage, have a slightly larger arc of movement. Another useful feature seldom found on small or medium size cars is a built-in hydraulically operated jacking system. This enables all four wheels to be jacked up or, alternatively, either the front or the rear end. It is operated by means of a detachable lever carried in the spare wheel compartment, which is applied to the pump and control unit under the bonnet.

Lighting

The head lights are particularly good for a car of this size and cover an adequate range and also give a good spread of light. The interior light is well placed and is controlled by a switch fitted in the roof above the right-hand front door, where it is unusually convenient. The instrument lighting is good and does not cause reflection in the windscreen. A heater of recirculating type was fitted to the car tested, but is not arranged for direct windscreen demisting or defrosting.

Both the Trafficator switch, of the time delay type, and the horn button are on the steering wheel hub, a less usual arrangement when rack and pinion steering is used. The horn note is reasonably effective but does not seem to be quite in keeping with the general quality character of the rest of the car. On two mornings during the test the car, standing in the open overnight, had some three inches of snow on roof and bonnet, but the engine fired instantly. In chilly weather a slight amount of splutter was experienced during the warm-up period unless the mixture control was kept in part use initially.

Considered as a whole, the 1¼-litre M.G. saloon is a very desirable car. It is light and lively, economical, handles well, has a good turn of speed and is handy in traffic and on narrow roads. It has a quality feel possessed by few small cars, and many desirable features found only on larger or more expensive products; it can carry four people and will hold a reasonable amount of luggage. It also has that air of a thoroughbred, brought about no doubt by its sporting ancestors that created the slogan " Safety Fast."